THE
taste
for living
COOKBOOK

Mike Milken's Favorite
Recipes for Fighting Cancer

The Association for the Cure of Cancer of the Prostate (CaP CURE)
1250 4th Street, Suite 360, Santa Monica, California 90401

A CaP CURE Book

Managing Editor: Joshua Mills
Food Editor: Lisa de Mauro
CaP CURE Scientific and Editorial Team:
Howard R. Soule, Ph.D., Chris Noxon, Erin Pasternack

Scientific Consultants: Donald S. Coffey, Ph.D., President, the American Association for Cancer Research,
Professor of Urology, Oncology, Pharmacology and Molecular Sciences, Johns Hopkins Hospital
David Heber, M.D., Ph.D., Director, UCLA Center for Human Nutrition,
Professor of Medicine, UCLA School of Medicine and Public Health,

Art Direction/Design: Joannah Ralston, Insight Design
Food Photographs: Bruce James, Lew Robertson, Burke/Triolo Productions
Location Photographs: Gary Moss
Hair & Makeup: Brenda Green for Celestine, L.A.
Food Styling: Norman Stewart, Janet Miller, Rick Ellis
Prop Styling: Lorraine Triolo, Burke/Triolo Productions
Illustrations: Isabelle Dervaux

Produced by
Allen & Osborne Inc.
148 State Street, Boston, Massachusetts 02109

10 9 8 7 6 5 4 3 2

Library of Congress Catalogue Card Number: 98-84838
Ginsberg, Beth
Milken, Mike
The Taste for Living Cookbook
Mike Milken's Favorite Recipes for Fighting Cancer

Includes index
ISBN 0-9660805-6-4
1. Cookbooks & Cookery. 2. Health & Fitness. 3. Medical/Nursing/Home Care

Cover Design: Joannah Ralston.
Cover Photographs: Bruce James, Lew Robertson, Gary Moss
Printed in USA

THE
taste
for living
COOKBOOK

Mike Milken's Favorite Recipes for Fighting Cancer

by Beth Ginsberg and Mike Milken

CaP CURE
ASSOCIATION FOR THE CURE
OF CANCER OF THE PROSTATE

CONTENTS

You'll swear this chocolate pudding is the real thing! page 46

A WORD ABOUT INGREDIENTS
AND NUTRITIONAL ANALYSIS

In recipes where a range of amounts is offered in the ingredients list ($\frac{3}{4}$ to 1 teaspoon of salt, for example), nutritional analysis is always based on the first amount. Similarly, if a choice of ingredients is offered ($\frac{1}{2}$ cup egg whites or egg substitute) the analysis is based on the first choice. Where an ingredient is listed as optional, it is not included in the nutritional analysis.

Tofu varies greatly from brand to brand; not every brand is available everywhere. For the purposes of our analysis, we used the tofu with the least amount of fat that we could find for the recipe. There may be slight variations in fat levels, depending on which tofu you use.

Garlic and onion powder may be used in place of granulated garlic and onion.

ACKNOWLEDGEMENTS

Thanks to Lance Toro, Marves White, Larry Hatfield
and Gus Rivas, for all their help, support and love.
To Lisa deMauro, Joannah Ralston and Josh Mills, for
lighting the fire, to Joel Kurtzman for making sure the
flame was always on high and to Jackie Collette, Karen
Vantrease, Kristen Croft, Erin Pasternack and Christopher
Noxon for keeping everything running smoothly.

To Mom, Merle Ginsberg and Dottie Witt for putting
up with me. To Charles Williams, Art Luna and Anastasia
Soare for always making me look good. Last but never
least, to Mike, for always allowing me to express myself
tastefully, giving me the encouragement to write this
book and for being in my life.

This book is dedicated to my daughter, Hannah.

INTRODUCTION

Mike Milken
Founder and Chairman, CaP CURE

WHEN your life is on the line, changing your diet can be easy. I know. When I was diagnosed with advanced prostate cancer in 1993 at the age of 46, I went from tuna melts and peanut butter to rice cakes and steamed broccoli overnight.

I didn't particularly enjoy my bland new diet. But I was determined to do everything in my power to beat cancer. That meant learning about the best of Western and Eastern medicine, making dramatic changes in my lifestyle and beginning to think of what I ate as an integral part of my recovery. I didn't care for dry baked potatoes or limp piles of steamed vegetables. However, the pleasure of eating was a small sacrifice for the pleasure of living. If a doctor could have given me a pill containing all the nutrients I needed to fight the disease, I would have gladly given up food forever.

But the cravings didn't stop.

While eating a bowl of lettuce with red-wine vinegar, my mind would invariably wander. I started craving chef's salads topped with Thousand Island dressing. I had incredibly vivid recollections of Caesar salads that my wife, Lori, and I had eaten during our courtship as college students. I missed the *joy of eating*.

In 1995, after consulting a number of scientists studying the role of diet and cancer, I went on a worldwide search for a chef who could incorporate nutritional research into food that I could actually enjoy.

The search led to Beth Ginsberg, an accomplished chef who specializes in healthy cuisine. Her cooking wasn't anything like what I had grudgingly come to accept as part of my recovery. Guided by the latest findings of scientists studying the link between diet and cancer, Beth created meals that tasted a lot like dishes I have always loved. Chili. Reuben sandwiches. Strawberry shortcake. It hardly seemed possible: I could eat well while undergoing nutrition therapy. I *could* have it both ways.

And so can you. The recipes in this book are designed to help you enjoy the pleasure of food while helping your body fight cancer. It is important to note that research on the role of diet in the progression of cancer is not yet conclusive. Researchers believe that wide global variations in the incidence of cancer are in part explained by differences in diet. But scientists are just beginning to understand how molecules in food and vitamins affect our bodies' cells and energize our bodies to fight cancer.

After five years of interacting with many of the world's leading scientists studying nutrition, I am increasingly convinced that it's not just what we eat in the typical American diet that puts us at a higher risk for cancer. It's also what we don't eat that contributes to the high incidence of cancer in the United States: one in two American men and one in three American women are diagnosed with cancer in their lifetime.

Like many of the estimated 11 million Americans living with cancer, I decided not to wait for rock-solid scientific evidence before changing my diet. Often we see relationships – the link between smoking and lung can-

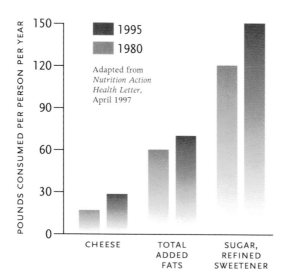

THE CHANGING AMERICAN DIET

Adapted from
*Nutrition Action
Health Letter,*
April 1997

POUNDS CONSUMED PER PERSON PER YEAR

■ 1995
□ 1980

CHEESE   TOTAL ADDED FATS   SUGAR, REFINED SWEETENER

cer, for instance – before scientists can document the exact molecular mechanisms that occur. Most important, I recognized that there is no harm, and probably a great deal of good, in beginning to eat low-fat foods rich in nutrients absent from the typical American diet.

....

I WAS born on July 4, 1946, during a period of unbridled optimism. Like many members of the Baby Boom generation, I was raised to believe that one person could make a difference and that any problem, no matter how difficult, could be solved if you put your mind to it. My parents provided a nurturing–but often quite rigorous–education.

At the dinner table, typically over such high-fat delicacies as fried chicken or brisket of beef, my brother and I had to be prepared to discuss any subject–the speed of light, the countries of the United Nations, social inequalities, balance sheets from my father's accounting clients, or the batting averages of major-league baseball players, past and present. Having dinner every night made for strong family bonding. But it wasn't exactly relaxing.

My choice for college was the University of California at Berkeley, for reasons both academic and personal. It was one of the top-rated universities in the country and had an internationally recognized faculty. More important, though, Berkeley represented a chance to see the world. Students came from all over to study, discuss and debate a dazzling

variety of ideas. After years of discussing the world at the dinner table, it seemed I could see it all just by walking across campus.

The university's academic excellence did not extend, however, to the local cuisine. While the intellectual climate could be quite avant garde, the food was absolutely mainstream. When a gourmet hot dog stand called Top Dog opened near campus in my junior year, it became the High Temple where we went to worship. Almost every night, my friends and I walked over to savor hot dogs or bratwurst on those fantastic buns. On a good night, I could eat a dozen at one sitting.

My diet wasn't just hot dogs. I became a star at breakfast eating contests in our fraternity kitchen. The contests were administered by a "chef" who thought of lard as one of the essential food groups. I would routinely put away 10 pancakes, 3 eggs over easy, 12 pieces of bacon, and cereal. I retired undefeated after reading about a college student who dropped dead after winning an eating contest. Weight was never a problem: I have an incredibly high metabolism. Even though I stopped for a giant hamburger and a large milkshake every day on the way home from classes, it wasn't until the third semester at Berkeley that I permanently broke the 150-pound barrier.

After Berkeley, my wife Lori and I moved to Philadelphia to attend graduate school. I soon developed a taste for some of the finer regional dishes, particularly Philly cheese steaks, and my own concoction of soft pretzels topped with peanut butter.

After graduating from the Wharton School, I began commuting to Wall Street, and a whole new set of eating habits began. On a typical morning, I hurried to catch the 5:30 a.m. bus for my 2-hour trip to New York. As I rushed through the kitchen, I grabbed one or two of my grandmother's buttery rolls, filled with nuts and raisins and topped with frosting.

By 1971, my life had changed substantially. I was 24, and running the research department at an investment firm. The work was invigorating. It provided opportunities to apply the theories I began developing on trips to visit my father's clients and later honed at Berkeley and Wharton. Once I reached the office I never left my desk. I ate breakfast and lunch—egg-and-bacon sandwiches, corned beef sandwiches, Chinese food, pizza—standing at the desk, often with two phones pressed to my ears.

By this time, technology was dramatically changing the way we worked. While the dramatic growth of CNN, MCI, Time Warner and the cable, cellular and health-care industries was still a few years off, innovations in technology were already beginning to have a profound impact not only on the economy, but on every other part of our lives. Intel had just introduced the first microchip, and Texas Instruments had just produced the first desktop electronic calculators.

I also remember reading that the President of the United

Michael and Lori Milken enjoying lunch outside their California home.

States had declared war on cancer. In a speech to the American people, he promised a cure within a decade. At the time, I had never known anyone with cancer and had given the disease little thought. My only memory was being a block captain for the American Cancer Society in elementary school.

By 1976, technology had advanced even further. NASA's Viking I spacecraft beamed back images of Mars. A team at MIT synthesized a functioning gene. And as our firm became a world leader in research and trading for industrial companies, we established links to offices around the world using computers and telecommunications. That same year the war on cancer reached the promised halfway point. Then, in early June, I learned that my father had been diagnosed with malignant melanoma.

I began traveling with him to cancer centers, looking for treatments that might help. I read about cancer. I talked to scientists. I learned all I could. For the first time I was confronting a problem that could not be solved – not by me, nor by any doctor or any scientist I called on. I moved back to California so my children, 5 and 2½ at the time, would have the chance to know their grandfather.

The relocation of my entire department to California had an unanticipated impact: I discovered a new world of food. I remember the first morning we arrived at 4:30 a.m. to prepare for the opening of the East Coast markets. By 7:30 a.m., the team of researchers, sales personnel and traders was starving but happy in the anticipation of our typical New York snack of greasy fast food and doughnuts. When the caterer wheeled in a trolley of brown wicker baskets brimming with vegetarian sandwiches on whole wheat bread, little cups of yogurt and bags of chopped veggies, he was almost devoured. He was lucky to get out alive.

By 1993, personal computers were in 31 million American homes. Fifty-eight million households were wired for cable. And 15 million Americans had become regular users of the Internet. As I attended an update on the Milken Family Foundation's cancer program, it struck me that the country had never made the moral or financial commitment necessary to bring the full promise of technology to bear on cancer. It had been 22 years since the President's declaration of war and another nine million Americans had died of cancer. I had lost my father, mother-in-law, stepfather, five other relatives and way too many friends.

That January, I had my first complete physical in two years. It was just a few weeks after one of my closest friends, Steve Ross, the chairman of Time Warner, had died of prostate cancer. Thinking of Steve, I asked my doctor to run a simple PSA test, one of the ways prostate cancer can be detected. He said I was too young to be tested.

"Humor me," I said.

And so I learned, in February 1993, that I had advanced prostate cancer. After consulting with researchers at a scientific conference in Houston and undergoing several weeks of additional tests, I discovered that my life expectancy was 12 to 18 months.

Because of my family history of cancer and our foundation's involvement in cancer research over the pre-

My father "might still be alive today if he had sought medical help earlier."

vious 17 years, I thought I understood cancer. I was astonished to learn that one in every five men will get prostate cancer. Prostate cancer appeared to be a "stealth" disease. It was not a major topic at scientific meetings, nor a priority on the national research agenda. I faced a crisis of uncertainty. No treatment option worked all the time. No medical expert could determine what would work best.

So many of my family and friends had lost their battles against cancer. What could I do that my relatives and friends had *not*? What could I do that would be different?

My father and Steve Ross had not taken time off to wage war on their disease. My dad worried about his clients and their problems and was slow to seek a diagnosis. He had not wanted to take time away from his work. He might still be alive today if he had sought medical help earlier. Steve was focused on his overriding vision, to build Time Warner into the most important entertainment company in the world. He didn't want his health to distract him.

I decided to shift my energy and concentration into changing my lifestyle and diet and taking charge of my own illness. A month after my diagnosis, I established CaP CURE, the Association for the Cure of Cancer of the Prostate. With the support of thousands of people, it has become the largest private funder of prostate cancer research.

INTERNATIONAL VARIATION IN PROSTATE CANCER INCIDENCE

ASIA
EASTERN EUROPE
SOUTH AMERICA
AUSTRALIA
EUROPE
GREENLAND
NORTH AMERICA

LOW
MEDIUM
HIGH

Since childhood, I had viewed life as a constant quest for knowledge. I set out to learn about Eastern medicine and ways to energize the world's greatest creation: the human body. It seemed clear that my health had suffered from all those years of eating fatty foods, all the meals eaten in haste and on the go, and more recently the stress from my legal problems.

My search for answers led to a meditation center in western Massachusetts that was based on the Ayurveda tradition of India. There Lori and I learned more about Eastern medicine, herbal cures and relaxation. We invited a doctor trained in both Western and Ayurveda medicine to move into our house for a few months. Early in the morning and late at night, we worked on breathing techniques, herbal therapy, meditation and yoga.

I learned how massage can activate the body's t-cells, which fight cancer, and how aromatherapy can energize the immune system. I rented a house at the beach and went for long walks. The smell of the seashore, and the water, brought back childhood memories of walks with my father at Lake Arrowhead in California.

Another benefit of the beach, I learned, was sunlight. Studies supported by CaP CURE show that sunlight and vitamin D help reduce the growth of prostate cancer. The studies also found a higher incidence of hormone-related cancers in northern Europe and the northern U.S. than in the southern parts of those continents. I thought back on all those long days in my windowless Wall Street office, and all those winter days I set off for work in darkness and returned in darkness. I had seen no more daylight than a hibernating bear.

After years of fielding a thousand calls a day, I turned off the phones in part of my house. And I changed how I ate. One

Ayurveda teaching was "Better to eat a stone sitting down than a meal standing up." Similarly, rabbinical law cautions against eating while standing. For someone who had eaten 2,000 to 3,000 meals standing at his desk, this was another chilling thought.

I decided to drastically reduce the fat in my diet, to 9 grams a day. I stopped eating meat, desserts and most dairy products. But that wasn't good enough. I found that even a single serving of "light" peanut butter exceeded my daily fat allowance. While I felt virtuous eating a mixed salad, I discovered that even a small amount of my favorite dressings put me way over the top. Even margarine that is 100 percent fat could legally be labeled "nonfat," so long as it contained less than one-half of 1 gram of fat per serving (Understanding Marketing Terms, page 42).

But cutting down on fat was not enough.

Research supported by CaP CURE showed that soy protein could be a critical missing ingredient. I learned that Americans have a five times higher incidence of prostate cancer than people living in Asia and eating a traditional Asian diet. These diets are typically rich in soy protein, which contains a nutrient called genistein. This chemical has been found in laboratories to interfere with the growth of prostate cancer cells and to inhibit angiogenesis, the new blood vessel growth required for tumor cells to spread throughout the body (page 44). *Genistein appears to help fight all hormonal cancers, including breast cancer.* Soy had never been a staple of my diet, but now I substituted tofu or tempeh for meat, and I began mixing soy protein isolate powder with water or fruit juice.

But until I found Beth Ginsberg, eating was more of a burden than a pleasure. Beth made it her mission to incorporate the latest scientific knowl-

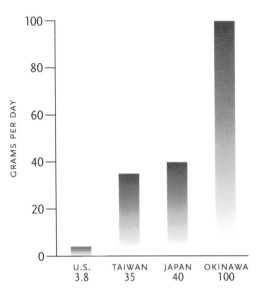

SOY PROTEIN INTAKE

GRAMS PER DAY

| U.S. | TAIWAN | JAPAN | OKINAWA |
| 3.8 | 35 | 40 | 100 |

edge in her adaptations of old, favorite recipes. Soon I was enjoying foods and flavors I had written off as long-lost memories. She turned my medicinal soy protein drinks into fruit smoothies that reminded me of the delicious Swiss orange-chip ice cream I would get at Swensen's Ice Cream in Berkeley (page 84). I could hardly guess that the drink was full of soy protein and other potential cancer-fighters like lemon and orange zest (the oils found in the skin contain limonene and geraniol, which have been shown to curtail tumor growth).

Even the hot dogs I had devoured as a college student made a comeback. Instead of red meat and who knows what else, these hot dogs are made of tofu. Beth even created a casserole using these hot dogs along with my beloved Philadelphia soft pretzels (page 42).

Beth reviewed scientific studies while formulating her recipes. When research supported by CaP CURE found that beans and lentils help lower levels of hormones that indicate prostate cancer risk, Beth found delicious ways to introduce these foods into my diet. When scientists reported that a chemical called lycopene found in cooked tomatoes seems to produce a reduced risk of prostate cancer, Beth added tomato paste to many recipes (page 17). After research on garlic and other allium vegetables indicated that they inhibit growth in a number of tumor cell lines, Beth increased the use of garlic as a seasoning. And finally, when scientists discovered that curcumin, which is found in cumin and is the yellow pigment found in turmeric, inhibits the development of certain cancers, Beth increased its use in chili (page 41) and employed it for coloring in a sauce in her version of Eggs Benedict (page 85).

One day I decided to really put my new diet and Beth to the test. I invited some colleagues to lunch. They were as far removed from the vegetarian crowd as you could get, and I wanted to see how they would react to one of my typical

"How do we teach our children to make changes NOW?"

meals. Beth served Reuben sandwiches (page 68), and afterwards I asked my guests what they thought they'd eaten. No one guessed that the cheese and Russian dressing were soy-based and the meat was actually tempeh. They all thought the sandwiches were delicious. I knew that if die-hard carnivores like these were convinced, we were on to something good.

. . . .

I WAS highly motivated to change my diet because I believed it could mean the difference between life and death. But I wondered: How do we teach our children to make changes now?

One answer might lie with science. Both skeptics and young people, I feel certain, will increasingly become convinced of the value of nutrition as science unlocks the secrets of the human body. I am confident that biology and chemistry will drive the scientific breakthroughs of the 21st century, just as the 20th century was shaped by physics and remarkable advances in engineering, mechanization, data storage and telecommunications.

As previous generations envisioned the future through the science fiction of Jules Verne, and my generation glimpsed it through "Star Trek," the children of today are just beginning to imagine no less remarkable innovations in biology. I am sure the day will come when our grandchildren will be as flabbergasted at how naive we are about the relationship between food and the human body as we are by our own grandparents' unease with such modern contraptions as the laptop computer and the cell phone.

While there is no magic formula or secret cure, I know that good health requires healthy eating. Thanks to scientists all over the world and to Beth Ginsberg, I have learned to make practical use of the latest nutritional research without giving up the joy of eating.

PREFACE

Beth Ginsberg

COOKING can be challenging for even the most experienced chef. It requires patience, thought, time and knowledge. But preparing great food that is good for you takes no more time or effort than cooking great food that's not—provided you have the right ingredients and use the right techniques.

This book will help you select the best ingredients and prepare them in the most nutritionally sound way. Flavor doesn't have to be lost when health is gained.

When I was growing up, I loved to eat and I was able to eat whatever I wanted without gaining weight. While studying art history and English literature, I began hosting dinner parties for my friends. With my love for eating and my interest in art, cooking became my creative outlet and my passion.

I was formally trained at the Culinary Institute of America, in Hyde Park, New York. But natural foods have always been part of my culinary repertoire. And when I moved to California my interest in health and sound nutrition grew. I developed a fresh-food line for Mrs. Gooch's Natural Food Markets and then started Naked Salads, a line of take-out fresh salads and dressings. I opened a small restaurant, called 442, that became a hangout for many of Hollywood's healthy eaters.

In August 1995, I went to work for Michael Milken as his personal and corporate chef. With his encouragement and with the latest nutritional data from CaP CURE, I became deeply immersed in health and nutrition and worked to develop a complete low-fat soy menu. I continue to adapt my recipes as new nutritional information emerges. Indeed, Michael provides the opportunity for me to work with some of the world's leading nutritionists, and I have been able to use my experience to help people diagnosed with various cancers or who have a family history of certain cancers.

One challenge has been to find ways to keep the food delicious while following principles of sound nutrition. I wander into health-foods store, looking for new ingredients—free of additives, preservatives, chemicals and dyes—that stimulate my imagination. Back in my kitchen, I turn on some music and transform these ingredients into dishes that will appeal to even the most sophisticated palates.

I particularly enjoy using natural ingredients to recreate American favorites like cream of tomato soup, lasagne, French fries, brownies and chocolate cake. My goal is to invent healthy versions of these dishes, without reducing their appeal.

Because I'm a single working mother, I know what it's like to come home from a hectic day and have to prepare a meal. I don't believe in foods that take days to prepare. I hope you will discover, as I have, that low-fat cuisine with tofu and soy can be easier to prepare than cooking with fats. Here are some ways I make my time in the kitchen easier:

Figure out what you're going to cook the night before and write yourself a "prep list." Make sure you'll have all the ingredients you need.

Feel free to alter a recipe or take it in a new direction.

Cooking should be creative and individual.

Make cooking a time of relaxation. Listen to music you love in your kitchen. You'll find that chopping, grating and puréeing can be therapeutic.

If you have children, encourage them to get involved. The more tasks I give my daughter to do, the better she gets at cooking—and the more fun she has in the kitchen. And that makes both of us feel good.

Changing your diet can be difficult. One tactic I recommend: if you're in a restaurant, at the movies or a party, don't be overwhelmed with guilt if you eat something that's not good for you. Being conscientious about good nutrition most of the time is what counts. Each day offers a new opportunity for healthy eating.

This book offers ways to change your eating habits, and your lifestyle, for the long term—without sacrificing the pleasure of delicious foods. It's not just for people worried about cancer. This book offers ways for everyone to celebrate life, by living healthfully and eating well.

TIPS FOR HEALTHIER EATING

Even if you aren't always able to stick to strictly low-fat dishes, you can use these techniques to raise the health value and lower the risk of the food you serve or eat.

Herbs and Spices: To make appetizing dishes with little or no fat, rely on granulated garlic or onion or appropriate herbs and spices. You'll get added flavor and, in some cases, added nutritional benefits (page 73).

Citrus Zest: Before you use the flesh of a citrus fruit, rinse the fruit to remove dirt or pesticides, then grate off the rind. The zest can add a fresh, tangy flavor to sweet sauces, desserts, chicken or fish. You can also blend it into a shake (page 84).

Soy Protein Isolate Powder: You can buy a low-fat soy powder made from isolate at many natural food stores or by mail order (page 111). Add it to cereal, ground meat dishes, dressings, sauces, shakes, soups or baked goods.

Cruciferous Vegetables: Broccoli, cabbage, Brussels sprouts or cauliflower make an excellent quick meal, dipped in mustard, salsa or yogurt, or served over a baked potato (page 78).

Green Tea: Serve green tea hot at the end of a meal, Japanese style. Or try it iced, flavored with mint and lemon zest. Drink 3 to 10 cups a day, because it contains valuable antioxidants. (Or add green tea powder to shakes, page 84.)

Salad Dressing and Mayonnaise: Avoid these. When dining out, ask for balsamic vinegar or lemon juice and mustard and stir together a healthy dressing at your table. Start with a salad of flavorful, dark green, leafy lettuce to reduce the need for salad dressing. Use mustard on sandwiches. Moisten tuna salad with lemon juice or vinegar and add onion, chopped peppers or pickles—anything that will add taste without fat.

Dairy Products: Stick with low-fat or nonfat milk and yogurt, but be aware that many of these products contain additives, so read labels carefully and shop in natural food stores whenever possible. Avoid sugar-rich yogurt and ice cream—including the nonfat kind—which will add calories and may tempt you to overindulge. Stay away from butter. Try fruit spreads on toast or waffles. Be aware that most cheese is 60 to 80 percent fat; dramatically reduce the amount you consume.

NUTRITIONAL PRINCIPLES OF CAP CURE

To fight prostate cancer and other hormonal cancers, CaP CURE recommends these principles of nutrition:
• Limit dietary fat to 15 percent of total energy intake.
• Eat 5 or more fruit and vegetable servings per day.
• Consume 25 to 35 grams of dietary fiber a day.
• Consume up to 40 grams of soy protein a day.

S O U P S

are made to

DELIGHT

the palate,

WARM the body,

and **SOOTHE**

the soul.

Nutritious and flavorful,

they are *truly* a healthy eater's best friend.

CORN CHOWDER WITH POPCORN CROUTONS

My favorite restaurant in Los Angeles is The Ivy. This is my nonfat version of its delicious soup. The popcorn croutons supply an added crunch.

CORN CHOWDER

1 **15-ounce can corn**

6 **cups fresh corn kernels, fresh or frozen** (*use a serrated knife to cut fresh kernels from cob; freeze stripped cobs for making Corn Broth*)

½ **cup celery, peeled and diced**

1 **large baking potato, peeled and diced (about 1½ cups)**

8 **cups Corn Broth, recipe follows** (*or substitute vegetable broth. Corn Broth gives a richer corn flavor*)

1 **teaspoon fresh or dried tarragon**

⅛ **teaspoon sea salt**

ground black pepper to taste

¼ **cup air-popped popcorn, for garnish**

TO MAKE CHOWDER

1. Puree canned corn with its liquid in a blender or food processor.

2. Place all ingredients, except popcorn, in a large soup pot and bring to a boil over medium high heat.

3. Turn down heat and let soup simmer until potatoes are tender, about 25 minutes, stirring occasionally.

4. Ladle into serving bowls and garnish each with a cluster of popcorn.

YIELD: 12 SERVINGS (3 QUARTS).

Per serving: 137 Calories, 0.7g Fat, 0.1g Saturated Fat, 0g Cholesterol, 4.2g Protein, 33g Carbohydrate, 3.7g Fiber, 171mg Sodium

CORN BROTH

15 **stripped corn cobs**

10-12 **cups water**

1. Place 15 corn cobs in a soup pot and cover with water. (Freeze all leftover cobs until you have enough to make broth. Corn Broth can also be frozen.)

2. Boil for 20 minutes.

3. Strain broth. You should have 8 cups. If not, return the broth to the pot and boil rapidly until you have 8 cups. Discard solids.

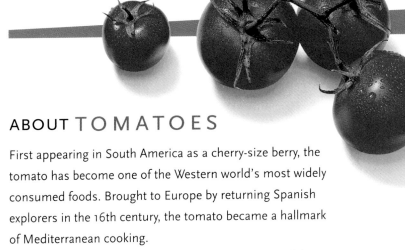

CREAM OF TOMATO SOUP

This is just like the soup Mama used to serve on a rainy day. Oats can be used as a cream replacement in any pureed soup.

- 2   28-ounce cans of low-sodium chopped tomatoes, including juice
- 7   cups Vegetable Stock (next page)
- 1   cup rolled oats
- 1   cup carrots, peeled and diced
- 3/4 cup celery, diced
- 2   teaspoons Tabasco Sauce, optional
- 1   teaspoon Spike seasoning or 1 teaspoon each dried basil and oregano
- 3/4 teaspoon sea salt
- 1/2 teaspoon ground black pepper, optional
- 36 nonfat oyster crackers, optional, for garnish

1. Place all ingredients except oyster crackers in a large soup pot over medium high heat.

2. Bring to a boil and turn down to a simmer. Cook about 25 to 35 minutes, stirring occasionally, until the vegetables have softened. If the mixture begins to stick to the bottom, change pots to avoid burning the soup.

3. Remove from heat and allow to cool slightly.

4. Puree in a blender or food processor in several batches, then return to a clean pot. Warm over low heat until just simmering.

5. Ladle into bowls. Float 3 nonfat oyster crackers on top of each serving.

YIELD: 12 SERVINGS (3 QUARTS)

Per serving: 81 Calories, 0.8g Fat,
0.1g Saturated Fat, 0g Cholesterol,
3g Protein, 17g Carbohydrate,
4g Fiber, 57mg Sodium

ABOUT TOMATOES

First appearing in South America as a cherry-size berry, the tomato has become one of the Western world's most widely consumed foods. Brought to Europe by returning Spanish explorers in the 16th century, the tomato became a hallmark of Mediterranean cooking.

Today the tomato provides more than 40 percent of the average American's vegetable consumption each year. That's very good news, because nowhere in nature does the substance lycopene appear in richer concentrations than in tomatoes.

An antioxidant, lycopene has been found to concentrate in the prostate gland, and it is believed to have some effects on prostate cells. While no scientific study has found that lycopene reduces prostate cancer growth, a study of 48,000 men conducted by Dr. Edward Giovannucci found that men who eat 10 or more servings a week of tomato-based foods are up to 45 percent less likely to develop prostate cancer.

Other studies in the United States and Germany found that consumption of tomato paste and other cooked tomato products increases the body's ability to absorb lycopene more than consumption of raw tomatoes. Other easy ways to consume lycopene are in ketchup and in tomato juice or vegetable-juice combinations that include tomato juice (only the low-sodium variety is recommended). Other studies have found that consumption of lycopene cuts the risk of cancer of the cervix, pancreas and digestive tract.

Lycopene is also found in watermelon and pink grapefruit.

VEGETABLE STOCK

To save time, buy fat-free vegetable stock or chicken broth instead of making your own.

- 4 medium carrots, peeled
- 4 stalks celery
- 2 onions, peeled
- 2 cloves garlic, peeled
- 1 leek
- 9 cups water

1. Cut carrots, celery and onions into rough chunks. Place in a large pot.

2. Add garlic to pot.

3. Cut leek in half lengthwise and rinse thoroughly to remove sand. Add to pot.

4. Add water and bring to a boil. Turn down to a simmer and cook for 25 minutes. Strain broth and reserve for soups and sauces. This keeps refrigerated up to 1 week and frozen up to 30 days.

YIELD: 7 CUPS

OLD-FASHIONED VEGETABLE BARLEY SOUP

For variety, you can substitute thin noodles for the barley. Add them along with the other ingredients.

- ¼ cup barley
- 10 cups Vegetable Stock (see left)
- 2 cups corn kernels, fresh or frozen
  (*use a serrated knife to cut fresh kernels from cob; freeze stripped cobs for making Corn Broth, page 16*)
- 1 14.5-ounce can low-sodium diced tomatoes, including juice
- 4 large carrots, cubed (about 2 cups)
- 1 large baking potato, peeled and cubed (about 1½ cups)
- ⅛ teaspoon sea salt
- 2 cups green beans

1. Rinse barley and drain.

2. Place all ingredients except green beans in a pot and heat over medium-high heat. Bring to a boil, then turn down to a simmer.

3. Cook for 30 minutes, stirring occasionally. Add green beans and cook until potatoes are tender and barley is soft, about 15 minutes more. Barley expands the longer it sits in liquid, so if soup becomes too thick add more water.

4. Ladle into bowls and serve.

YIELD: 12 SERVINGS (3 QUARTS)

Per serving: 112 Calories, 0.3g Fat, 0.1g Saturated Fat, 0g Cholesterol, 3.1g Protein, 26g Carbohydrate, 4.4g Fiber, 78mg Sodium

ZUCCHINI SOUP WITH ROASTED RED PEPPER

- 1 cup sliced onions (about 1 medium)
- 6 cups sliced zucchini (about 5 medium)
- 1 Roasted Red Pepper, diced (see below)
- 6 cups Vegetable Stock (page 18)
- ½ cup rolled oats
- ⅛ teaspoon sea salt
  - black pepper, to taste
  - canola oil cooking spray

1. Spray a large soup pot once with cooking spray. Place over low flame. Add onion and cook until browned, about 3 minutes, stirring frequently. Add zucchini and ¼ of the diced red pepper. Cover and cook until vegetables are tender, about 15 minutes.

2. Add vegetable stock. Stir in oats and ½ of the diced pepper. Bring to a boil, lower to a simmer and cook until oats are creamy, about 25 minutes, stirring occasionally.

3. After soup cools slightly, puree in a blender or food processor, then return to pot. Reheat gently. Add salt and black pepper to taste.

4. Garnish with reserved diced pepper.

YIELD: 8 SERVINGS (2 QUARTS)

Per serving: 85 Calories, 0.5g Fat, 0.1g Saturated Fat, 0g Cholesterol, 2.9g Protein, 19g Carbohydrate, 3.6g Fiber, 93mg Sodium

ROASTED RED PEPPER

Place pepper directly in the flame of a burner, on a grill or under the broiler. Turn pepper until it blackens and blisters on all sides. Transfer to a bowl and cover for 10 minutes. Hold pepper under running water as you peel off loosened skin and remove seeds.

FRENCH ONION SOUP

Serve this soup with or without the bubbling soy cheese topping.

- 6 large onions, peeled and halved lengthwise, cut into thin slices (about 9 cups)
- 1 tablespoon mirin, Madeira or Marsala
- 9 cups Vegetable Stock (page 18)
- 2 tablespoons low-sodium tamari soy sauce
- ½ teaspoon fresh thyme or ⅛ teaspoon dried
- 10 slices nonfat bread, crusts removed
- 1¼ pounds nonfat mozzarella-style soy cheese, cut into ½" slices (about 2½ cups)
  - canola oil cooking spray
- 2 green onions, chopped, for garnish

1. Spray a soup pot once with cooking spray. Place over a low flame. Add onions and cook until golden brown, stirring occasionally.

2. Stir in mirin, Vegetable Stock, tamari sauce and thyme. Bring to a boil and turn down to a simmer. Cook for about 45 minutes.

3. Preheat oven to 325°. Place bread slices on a baking sheet and toast in oven until bread is a golden color.

4. When soup is ready, ladle into ovenproof bowls. Float 1 toast slice on top of each serving. Cover with cheese.

5. Place filled bowls in oven for 5 minutes to melt cheese. Remove soup and set oven to broil. Place bowls under broiler to lightly brown cheese. (*Soy cheese, unlike conventional cheese, won't brown and melt in 1 step.*)

6. Garnish with chopped green onions and serve.

YIELD: 10 SERVINGS (2½ QUARTS)

Per serving: 276 Calories, 1.3g Fat, 0.3g Saturated Fat, 0.3 g Cholesterol, 19.5g Protein, 43g Carbohydrate, 4g Fiber, 790mg Sodium

BROCCOLI POTATO SOUP

For Broccoli Cheddar soup, add 1 cup grated nonfat cheddar-style soy cheese after pureeing soup. To jazz it up a bit, add a Roasted Red Pepper (page 20) to the soup while it's cooking.

- 1 head broccoli (about 1 pound), rinsed, lightly trimmed and cut into large chunks
- 2 medium potatoes, peeled and cut into chunks (about 2 cups)
- 7 cups Vegetable Stock (page 18)
- ⅛ teaspoon sea salt
- black pepper to taste

1. Put all ingredients in soup pot.

2. Place over high heat and bring to a boil. Reduce heat to a simmer and cook until potatoes are soft, about 25 minutes. Remove from heat and purée the soup in batches in a blender or food processor, then return to the pot.

3. Reheat before serving.

YIELD: 8 SERVINGS (2 QUARTS)

Per serving: 88 Calories, 0.1g Fat, 0g Saturated Fat, 0g Cholesterol, 3.9g Protein, 19g Carbohydrate, 3.8g Fiber, 31mg Sodium

SHIITAKE MISO SOUP *(photo on page 44)*

This is a delicious light soup. To make it even lighter—and more elegant—serve Shiitake Miso Consommé, minus the carrots and tofu. If you plan to freeze this soup, don't add the miso until you are ready to serve it; stir in 1 teaspoon of miso for each 1-cup serving.

- 4 cups shiitake mushrooms
- 3 carrots (about 1½ cups)
- 1 cup low-fat silken tofu, in ¼" dice (8 ounces)
- 8 cups water
- ¼ cup low-sodium tamari sauce
- ⅛ teaspoon granulated garlic
- ¼ cup white miso paste
- 4 green onions, sliced thin, for garnish

1. Remove stems from shiitake mushrooms. (*You can freeze the stems to use when making Vegetable Stock.*)

2. Slice mushrooms into ¼" strips. Rinse them and place in a soup pot.

3. Peel carrots and slice in half lengthwise and then into ¼" slices widthwise (*to make "half moon" slices*). Add to the soup pot along with the tofu.

4. Add water, tamari sauce and granulated garlic. Place over high heat until mixture come to a boil. Turn down to a simmer, cover and allow to cook for 20 minutes. Remove the pot from the heat.

5. Add miso and stir until it dissolves. (*Never boil miso soup. Just warm over low heat stirring occasionally. The miso contains valuable enzymes that are destroyed by boiling.*)

6. Ladle hot soup into bowls and sprinkle with green onions.

YIELD: 12 SERVINGS (3 QUARTS)

Per serving: 47 Calories, 0.7g Fat, 0.1g Saturated Fat, 0g Cholesterol, 3.5g Protein, 7g Carbohydrate, 1.9g Fiber, 409mg Sodium

EXERCISE

LACK of exercise can be as dangerous as poor diet. Yet to an alarming degree, too many people live as sedentary creatures.

A beginning exercise program does not require radical changes in routines, and changes do not need to be made overnight. In between the extremes of couch potato and marathon runner are hundreds of activities that work your muscles, heart and lungs. Get involved in exercise that grows out of daily routines—vacuum more frequently (burns 120 calories in a half-hour), tend your garden (390 calories in an hour), wash your car by hand, walk a little more by parking farther from your destination.

Exercise does not need to be especially vigorous to be beneficial, advises the 1996 Report on Physical Activity and Health from the Surgeon General. The report recommends that everyone get 30 minutes of moderate physical activity every day.

Walk young children to school; when they're old enough, have them walk by themselves. If you commute by train or bus, try walking to and from the station. Bowling (burns 190 calories in an hour), golf without a cart, ballroom dancing—all these add exercise to your life. You don't need a personal trainer, a fancy outfit or expensive lessons.

Even modest exercise can help:
- lower blood pressure
- lower the risk of some cancers
- lower the risk of heart disease
- lower insulin levels
- keep extra weight off

Exercise may also reduce the pain of arthritis and may relieve depression.

Exercise is a broad category. It includes *stretching*, which keeps your joints and muscles loose and limber; *strengthening*, which lowers LDL (low-density lipoproteins, the "bad" cholesterol), while building muscles and strengthening bones; and *aerobic exercise*, which burns fat, strengthens the heart and lungs and raises the levels of HDL (high-density lipoproteins, the "good" cholesterol).

Weight control is important because research has concluded that body fat is a storage area for substances that could cause cancer. For nonsmokers, the principal threats to men are prostate cancer and colon cancer, to women breast cancer and colon cancer. Reducing body fat has been found to reduce the risk of these cancers.

It's never too late to start exercising and enjoying its benefits. Studies of frail people 86 to 96 years old have shown they can strengthen their muscles, become more mobile, steadier on their feet and more self-sufficient. Many weaknesses that we associate with aging are in fact the cumulative effects of lack of exercise.

And it's never too early: get your children and grandchildren exercising, too.

a d s

are FUN.

They combine

FRESH flavors,

bright colors,

and PLAYFUL textures

on the plate.

Eat them every day.

TACO SALAD IN A CHILI LIME DRESSING

over 60 minutes

To make tacos, fold a fat-free tortilla in half and bake at 350° until crunchy. Stuff with the vegetarian taco "meat" mix and top with shredded lettuce, tomatoes and soy cheese.

SALAD

- ½ cup dried black beans (2 cups cooked) or use 1 15-ounce can black beans, rinsed
- 4 ears corn
- 1 small jicama, optional
- 1 red pepper, diced
- ½ bunch chopped cilantro
- 9 fat-free wheat tortillas
- ¼ teaspoon chili powder
- 1 head romaine lettuce
- 1 recipe Chili Lime Dressing (next page)
- 1 bunch green onions, sliced, for garnish

TACO MEAT

- 1 onion, peeled and diced
- 1½ pounds soy "meat" (*in the form of fat-free burgers or fat-free ground vegetarian meat*)
- 1 15-ounce can diced low-sodium tomatoes, including juice
- 1 teaspoon diced canned chilies, or more to taste
- 1 teaspoon ground cumin
- 1 teaspoon chili powder
- ½ teaspoon granulated garlic
- ¼ teaspoon granulated onion
- canola oil cooking spray

TO MAKE SALAD

1. Rinse dried black beans in a colander. Transfer beans to a large pot and cover with water. Bring water to a boil over medium high heat. Then turn down, keeping water at the boil, until beans are tender but not mushy, about 1¼ hours. Drain and refrigerate beans at least 30 minutes. (*Beans may be prepared up to this point and refrigerated for 24 hours.*)

2. Preheat oven to 350°.

3. Bring a pot of water to a boil and blanch corn for 2 minutes. Remove ears and strip kernels from cob using a serrated knife. Transfer kernels to a large bowl.

4. Peel jicama and cut into small cubes. Add to bowl.

5. Add black beans, red pepper and cilantro to the bowl with the corn. Cover and refrigerate.

6. Spray a baking sheet once with cooking spray. Cut 3 tortillas into matchstick-size strips. Place on prepared baking sheet.

7. Sprinkle strips with chili powder.

8. Bake in preheated oven until golden brown, about 15 minutes. Transfer strips to a bowl and set aside.

9. Rinse and dry romaine, discarding dark green leaves.

10. Shred romaine with a knife and refrigerate until ready to use.

TO PREPARE "MEAT" AND TORTILLAS

1. Preheat oven to 350° degrees.

2. Spray a sauté pan once with cooking spray. Add diced onions and cook over low heat until tender, stirring occasionally, about 5 minutes. Add soy "meat" and break it up with a spoon.

3. Add tomatoes, chilies, cumin, chili powder, garlic and onion. Cook, stirring occasionally, for 5 minutes. Remove from heat.

4. Spread out remaining tortillas over racks in preheated oven until crispy and golden brown, about 8 to 10 minutes. Place 1 tortilla on each of 6 plates.

TO COMPLETE SALAD

1. Toss romaine with 2 tablespoons Chili Lime Dressing. Divide the romaine among the tortillas.

2. Toss vegetables with remaining dressing and spoon over lettuce.

3. Place a small mound of prepared "meat" in the center of the vegetables and stick the matchstick tortilla strips in the center of the "meat" so that they stand up and fan out.

4. Sprinkle with green onions and serve.

YIELD: **6** SERVINGS

Per serving: 483 Calories, 2g Fat, 0.3g Saturated Fat, 0g Cholesterol, 33.2g Protein, 86g Carbohydrate, 17.3g Fiber, 1306mg Sodium

CHILI LIME DRESSING

Make lemon vinaigrette by substituting fresh lemon juice for the lime juice and omitting the chili powder.

- 1 **cup low-sodium tamari soy sauce**
- 1 **cup mirin (sweetened Japanese rice wine)**
- ½ **cup brown rice vinegar** (*you may substitute white*)
  juice from 4 limes (about ⅔ cup)
- 2 **teaspoons granulated onion**
- 1 **teaspoon chili powder**
- 1 **teaspoon grated lime zest**

1. Place all in ingredients in a bowl and stir together.

2. This dressing will keep up to 2 weeks stored in a glass container in the refrigerator.

YIELD: **2½** CUPS

Per tablespoon: 9 Calories, 0g Fat, 0g Saturated Fat, 0g Cholesterol, 0.8g Protein, 1g Carbohydrate, 0.1g Fiber, 280mg Sodium

CAESAR SALAD WITH HERB CROUTONS

A remake of the classic, this is best served in a wooden bowl and garnished with fresh herb croutons.

CROUTONS

1 fat-free baguette, cut into ½" slices, or a loaf of fat-free bread

2 tablespoons chopped fresh basil or 1 tablespoon dried

1 tablespoon chopped fresh rosemary (*if available*)

1 tablespoon chopped fresh parsley

1 teaspoon granulated garlic

canola oil cooking spray, preferably garlic-flavored

SALAD

1 head romaine lettuce

1 cup herb croutons (see below)

1 tablespoon parmesan-style soy cheese

½ cup Caesar salad dressing (next page)

TO MAKE CROUTONS

1. Preheat oven to 350°.

2. Cut bread slices into 1" squares with a serrated knife. Place squares in a bowl.

3. Add basil, rosemary, parsley and garlic to bowl and toss well.

4. Spray a baking sheet once with cooking spray. Place croutons on sheet and bake in preheated oven until croutons are light brown, about 20 minutes. Use right away or cool to store.

5. These will keep up to 1 month if stored in an airtight container.

TO MAKE SALAD

1. Wash romaine, dry by patting with paper towels or in a salad spinner and tear into bite-size pieces. (*Tearing lettuce, rather than cutting with a knife, keeps it from turning brown at the edges.*)

2. Place lettuce, croutons, soy cheese and dressing in a bowl and toss. Serve.

YIELD: 4 SERVINGS

Per serving: 51 Calories, 0.6g Fat, 0.2g Saturated Fat, 0g Cholesterol, 2.1g Protein, 8g Carbohydrate, 2.7g Fiber, 104mg Sodium

CAESAR DRESSING

- 1 clove garlic, peeled
  (should equal ¹/₂ teaspoon chopped)
- ¹/₂ cup low-fat silken tofu (4 ounces)
- ¹/₃ cup water
- ¹/₄ cup fresh lemon juice
- 1 tablespoon white miso paste
- 2 teaspoons Dijon mustard
- 1 tablespoon parmesan-style soy cheese
  or whey powder
- 1¹/₂ teaspoons granulated garlic
- 1 teaspoon granulated onion
- ¹/₄ teaspoon cracked black pepper
- ¹/₄ teaspoon Worcestershire sauce

1. Place garlic in a food processor fitted with a metal blade and chop fine.

2. Scrape down sides of work bowl. Add remaining ingredients and process until smooth.

3. Dressing will keep up to 4 days stored in a glass container in the refrigerator. If it thickens, add a little water to thin it.

YIELD: 1 CUP

Per tablespoon: 8 Calories, 0.2g Fat, 0.1g Saturated Fat, 0g Cholesterol, 0.8g Protein, 1g Carbohydrate, 0.2g Fiber, 50mg Sodium

ABOUT GARLIC

Long before literature and folk tales accorded garlic the power to ward off vampires, ancient Egyptians worshipped garlic and Greek athletes chewed it for good luck. Scientists have now concluded what myth first implied: consumption of garlic has medicinal benefits.

Precisely why garlic affects tumor growth is not known, but garlic has been shown, in numerous studies, to limit growth in a number of tumor cell lines by inhibiting signals for cell proliferation. Researchers suspect that garlic deactivates enzymes needed for cancer cells to replicate.

Epidemiological studies in China and Italy have also found a greatly reduced risk of stomach cancer in people whose diet is rich in garlic.

Garlic contains a number of organosulfur compounds that have been associated with lower incidence of gastric and colorectal cancers. One extract of garlic is allyl sulfide, which is similar in chemical structure to glutathione, a natural antioxidant made in our bodies. Researchers are also studying whether the other allium vegetables—onion, leek, shallot and chives—bring similar benefits.

SPINACH SALAD WITH CRISPY ONIONS IN A SWEET ONION DRESSING

This is a take-off on Spinach Salad with Crispy Bacon. The Sweet Onion Dressing also makes a great marinade for chicken, fish, tofu and vegetables.

1 cup mushrooms

2 bunches spinach, well-rinsed, trimmed and dried, or 1 bag of washed baby spinach

1 cup cherry tomatoes

1 cup Sweet Onion Dressing (next page)

1 recipe Crispy Onion Rings (next page)
canola oil cooking spray

1. Cut mushrooms in quarters and rinse to remove any dirt.

2. Spray a sauté pan with cooking spray and cook mushrooms over low heat until just soft, about 3 minutes. Remove from heat.

3. Wash cherry tomatoes and cut in half lengthwise.

4. Place spinach, mushrooms and cherry tomatoes in a large salad bowl and toss with dressing.

5. Place portions of salad on plates and garnish with Crispy Onion Rings.

YIELD: **4** SERVINGS

Per serving: 279 Calories, 1.3g Fat, 0.2g Saturated Fat, 0g Cholesterol, 7g Protein, 51g Carbohydrate, 8.1g Fiber, 1000mg Sodium

CRISPY ONION RINGS

If you plan to serve these as a side dish
instead of a garnish, you might want to double the recipe.

- 2 onions, peeled
- ¾ cup all-purpose flour
- ½ cup nonfat egg substitute
- ¾ cup nonfat bread crumbs
- 1 teaspoon dried oregano
- 1 teaspoon dried basil
- 1½ teaspoons granulated garlic
- 1½ teaspoons granulated onion
- ½ teaspoon sea salt

1. Preheat oven to 400°. Spray a baking sheet once with cooking spray. Set aside.

2. Slice onions widthwise. Break apart into individual rings.

3. Line up 3 mixing bowls. Into the first, put the flour. Into the second, put the egg substitute. In the third, mix together the bread crumbs, herbs, spices and salt.

4. Dip each onion ring into the flour, then into the egg substitute and finally into the bread-crumbs. Place on prepared baking sheet.

5. When you have assembled all the onion rings on the sheet, bake in the preheated oven until rings are crispy and light brown, about 20 minutes. (*You can freeze the prepared onions before they're baked, then bake when needed.*)

YIELD: 4 SERVINGS

Per serving: 196 Calories, 0.4g Fat, 0.1g Saturated Fat, 0g Cholesterol, 8.4g Protein, 39g Carbohydrate, 2.5g Fiber, 509mg Sodium

SWEET ONION DRESSING

You can substitute roasted onions (page 76) for the raw ones in this recipe and skip the sautéing step.

- 2 large onions, peeled
- ½ cup balsamic vinegar
- ½ cup mirin (sweetened Japanese rice wine)
- ½ cup low-sodium tamari soy sauce
- 1 teaspoon granulated onion
  canola oil cooking spray

1. Slice onions lengthwise and then cut the slices into thin slivers.

2. Spray a sauté pan once with cooking spray. Add onions and cook over low heat until onions are softened and light brown, stirring occasionally, about 10 minutes.

3. Place cooked onions, vinegar, mirin, tamari sauce and granulated onion in a food processor fitted with a metal blade or in a blender and puree.

4. This dressing will keep for 1 week, tightly covered, in the refrigerator. A glass container is recommended for keeping it fresh.

YIELD: 2 CUPS

Per tablespoon: 15 Calories, 0g Fat, 0g Saturated Fat, 0g Cholesterol, 0.6g Protein, 2g Carbohydrate, 0.2g Fiber, 176mg Sodium

CHINESE ROASTED TOFU SALAD

- 1" piece fresh ginger, peeled
- 2 small cloves garlic, peeled
- ½ cup honey
- ½ cup low-sodium tamari soy sauce
- 1 tablespoon cornstarch
- 2 cups low-fat firm tofu (1 pound)
- ¼ head green cabbage
- ¼ head red cabbage
- 1 romaine lettuce heart, rinsed, dried and shredded
- 2 carrots, peeled and shredded
- 1 cup mung bean sprouts
- 1 bunch green onions, chopped
- 10 fat-free egg roll wrappers
- ½ recipe Orange Ginger Dressing (see right)
  canola oil cooking spray

1. Place garlic and ginger in a food processor fitted with a metal blade and chop fine. Scrape down sides of work bowl. Add honey, tamari sauce and cornstarch. Process until thoroughly blended.

2. Cut tofu into ½" cubes and place in bowl. Pour tamari mixture over tofu and allow to marinate at least 30 minutes (*or as long as overnight for a richer flavor*).

3. Preheat oven to 350°. Place tofu on a baking sheet and bake until marinade thickens and tofu is a light brown color, about 35 to 45 minutes. Transfer tofu to a bowl and set aside until ready to use. Do not turn off oven.

4. Spray a baking sheet once with cooking spray. Cut egg roll wrappers into matchstick-size strips and place on baking sheet. Bake until golden brown, about 20 minutes. Remove from oven and set aside.

5. Shred cabbages in a food processor fitted with a shredding blade or by hand for a better appearance. Place cut head flat-side down on a cutting board. Slice into thin strips. Transfer to a bowl.

6. Add romaine and carrots to bowl along with bean sprouts and green onions. Add about ⅔ of the crispy egg roll sticks to the bowl, pour in ½ cup Orange Ginger dressing and toss to mix thoroughly. (*For a more elegant presentation, arrange the ingredients separately.*)

7. Place ⅙ of the salad mixture on a plate. Spoon ⅙ of the tofu on top. Poke some crispy wonton sticks into the tofu so that they stand up. Sprinkle with chopped green onions over all. (*Serve reserved dressing on the side.*)

YIELD: 6 SERVINGS

Per serving: 313 Calories, 2.7g Fat, 0.3g Saturated Fat, 2.8g Cholesterol, 14.9g Protein, 59g Carbohydrate, 5.8g Fiber, 1842mg Sodium

ORANGE GINGER DRESSING

- 2" piece fresh ginger, peeled
- 1 shallot, peeled (about 1 tablespoon chopped)
- 1 cup canned mandarin orange segments, including juice
- ¼ cup low-sodium tamari soy sauce
- 2 tablespoons water
- 1 tablespoon white miso paste
- 1 teaspoon grated orange zest
- ¼ teaspoon granulated garlic

1. Place ginger and shallot in a food processor fitted with a metal blade and chop fine.

2. Scrape down the sides of the work bowl. Add remaining ingredients and blend. (*Dressing will keep up to 4 days stored in a glass container in the refrigerator.*)

YIELD: ABOUT 2 CUPS

Per tablespoon: 11 Calories, 0g Fat, 0g Saturated Fat, 0g Cholesterol, 0.6g Protein, 1g Carbohydrate, 0g Fiber, 204mg Sodium

CHEF'S SALAD WITH THOUSAND ISLAND DRESSING, MISO SHALLOT DRESSING OR RASPBERRY VINAIGRETTE

under 30 minutes

This salad may make you nostalgic for cafeteria meals of your past. Naturally any dressing in this chapter can be used on this salad—and on any salad. The choice is yours.

4	eggs
1	pound assorted soy deli slices (such as fat-free tofu bologna, ham, turkey or smoked tofu)
1	romaine lettuce heart, rinsed and dried
2	carrots, peeled and shredded
1/4	head red cabbage, shredded
8	ounces fat-free soy cheese (about 1 cup)
1/2	green pepper, sliced into 1/4" rings
1/2	red pepper, sliced into 1/4" rings
1/2	yellow pepper, sliced into 1/4" rings
4	Roma or other vine-ripened tomatoes, quartered
1	cup salad dressing: Thousand Island, Miso Shallot or Raspberry Vinaigrette (all on next page)

1. Place eggs in a saucepan and cover with water. Bring to a boil over medium heat, remove from heat, cover pan and allow to sit for 12 minutes. Remove eggs and cool them in cold water.

2. Peel eggs and cut in half lengthwise. Discard yolks (*or save them to feed your pet*) and rinse egg white gently under cool water to remove any yolk particles. Slice in half again (*to make quarters*) and set aside.

3. Cut deli slices and soy cheese into baton-size strips (about 1/4" wide) and set aside.

4. Tear romaine leaves into bite-sized pieces. Place in a bowl. Add carrots and cabbage to bowl and toss well.

5. Divide romaine mixture among 4 plates.

6. Mound soy cheese strips on 2 facing sides of the lettuce mound. Mound deli slices on the other 2 facing sides. Place 1 ring each of green, red and yellow pepper on top of the lettuce mixture (*in the middle of the cheese and "meat" batons*). Place egg white quarters and tomato quarters alternating around the edge.

7. Serve 1/4 cup dressing on the side with each salad.

YIELD: 4 SERVINGS

Per serving: 306 Calories, 0.4g Fat, 0g Saturated Fat, 0g Cholesterol, 47.7g Protein, 27.5g Carbohydrate, 6.1g Fiber, 1465mg Sodium

THOUSAND ISLAND DRESSING

- 1 **shallot, peeled** (about 1 tablespoon chopped)
- 1 **dill pickle or 1 tablespoon fat-free pickle relish**
- 1 **cup ketchup**
- 3/4 **cup low-fat silken tofu (6 ounces)**
- 3/4 **cup water**
- 1 **tablespoon granulated onion**

1. Place shallot and pickle in a food processor fitted with a metal blade and process. (*Ingredients may splat against the walls of the work bowl and not get completely processed. They'll blend in during step 2.*)

2. Scrape down sides of work bowl. Add remaining ingredients and process until pureed.

3. Transfer dressing to a covered container and refrigerate. A glass container is recommended for keeping the dressing fresh longest. It should keep for 3 to 4 days. If it thickens, add a little water and shake jar.

YIELD: 2 CUPS

Per tablespoon: 8 Calories, 0g Fat, 0g Saturated Fat, 0g Cholesterol, 0.5g Protein, 2g Carbohydrate, 0.2g Fiber, 58mg Sodium

MISO SHALLOT DRESSING

- 1 **cup honey**
- 1/2 **cup Dijon mustard**
- 1/2 **cup brown rice vinegar** (*you may substitute white*)
- 1/4 **cup white miso paste**
- 1/4 **cup water**
- 1 **shallot, peeled** (about 1 tablespoon chopped)
- 1 **teaspoon low-sodium tamari soy sauce**
- 1/4 **teaspoon ground black pepper, optional**

1. Place all ingredients in a food processor fitted with a metal blade or in a blender and process. (*Dressing will keep up to 1 week in a glass container in the refrigerator.*)

YIELD: 2 1/2 CUPS

Per tablespoon: 29 Calories, 0.1g Fat, 0g Saturated Fat, 0g Cholesterol, 0.2g Protein, 7g Carbohydrate, 0.1g Fiber, 95mg Sodium

RASPBERRY VINAIGRETTE

- 1 **shallot, peeled** (about 1 tablespoon chopped)
- 3/4 **cup frozen raspberries**
- 1/2 **cup liquid fruit sweetener, apple juice concentrate or honey**
- 1/4 **cup raspberry vinegar**
- 1 **tablespoon Dijon mustard**
- 1/8 **teaspoon sea salt**

1. Place shallot in a food processor fitted with a metal blade and process. Scrape down sides of work bowl. Add remaining ingredients and process. (*Dressing will keep up to 5 days in a glass container in the refrigerator.*)

YIELD: 1 1/4 CUPS

Per tablespoon: 31 Calories, 0.1g Fat, 0g Saturated Fat, 0g Cholesterol, 0.2g Protein, 8g Carbohydrate, 0.7g Fiber, 25mg Sodium

CHOPPED VEGETABLE SALAD WITH HONEY MUSTARD DRESSING

This is a crunchy, fresh-tasting dish. In the summer, try serving it with grilled scallops, chicken or tofu. Use the Honey Mustard Dressing as a sauce on steamed broccoli or cabbage or baked potatoes—it's versatile and delicious.

> 2 ears corn
> 1 cup Edemame (frozen green soybeans)
> 1 cup peas, fresh or frozen
> 2 carrots, peeled
> 2 stalks celery, trimmed
> 1 red bell pepper, trimmed and seeded
> ½ pound mixed salad greens, rinsed and dried, if necessary
> 1 cup Honey Mustard Dressing

1. Bring a pot of water to a boil, add corn and cook for 2 minutes. Remove from water and rinse under cold water.

2. Strip kernels from corn cob using a serrated knife. Place kernels in a bowl.

3. Use the same pot of boiling water to cook soybeans for 20 minutes. Shuck soybeans and add to the bowl with the corn.

4. In the same pot of boiling water cook peas until they are just tender, about 3 to 5 minutes. Remove from water and rinse under cold water. Add to the bowl containing the corn.

5. Dice carrots, celery and red pepper into small cubes about the size of corn kernels. Add to the bowl of corn.

6. Add ½ cup Honey Mustard Dressing to the mixed vegetables and toss.

7. In a separate bowl, toss salad greens with the remaining dressing.

8. Divide the lettuce evenly among 6 plates. Mound equal portions of the vegetables over the lettuce.

YIELD: 6 SERVINGS

Per serving: 335 Calories, 10.6g Fat, 1.4g Saturated Fat, 0g Cholesterol, 20.5g Protein, 47g Carbohydrate, 10.7g Fiber, 449mg Sodium

HONEY MUSTARD DRESSING

> 1 shallot peeled (about 1 tablespoon chopped)
> 1½ cup Dijon mustard
> ¾ cup honey
> ¼ cup raspberry vinegar or brown or white rice vinegar
> ¼ cup water
> 1 tablespoon granulated onion

1. Place shallot in a food processor fitted with a metal blade and purée.

2. Scrape down sides of work bowl. Add remaining ingredients and process.

3. Refrigerate in a glass container up to 1 week. If you wish to keep this dressing longer, prepare it without the shallot. Add the shallot when you are ready to use the dressing.

YIELD: 2 CUPS

Per tablespoon: 33 Calories, 0.5g Fat, 0g Saturated Fat, 0g Cholesterol, 0.6g Protein, 7g Carbohydrate, 0.3g Fiber, 147mg Sodium

e n t r

offer
SAVORY
POSSIBILITIES...
from
down-home  favorites

TO THE **ULTIMATE**
*in Haute
Cuisine.*

TERIYAKI TOFU BOWL WITH CHINESE VEGETABLES

There's plenty of room for improvisation in this recipe. You can add your favorite vegetables and eliminate any you don't like or can't find—just keep the overall quantity close to the amounts listed. If you prefer, purchase a fat-free, additive-free teriyaki sauce instead of making your own.

- 2 pounds or 2 blocks low-fat firm tofu (4 cups)
- 1 recipe Teriyaki Sauce (see below)
- 2 cups mushrooms
- 1 cup raw jasmine or brown basmati rice
- 1 red pepper, diced into 1/2" pieces
- 1 head broccoli (about 1 pound), trimmed and cut into florets
- 3 medium zucchini, sliced lengthwise and then cut into 1/4" slices
- 3 large carrots, slice lengthwise and then cut into 1/4" slices
- 1/2 bunch bok choy, cut into 1/2" slices (about 2 cups)
- 3 tablespoons fresh ginger, peeled and grated (about 3" piece)
- 2 tablespoons crushed fresh garlic
- 2 cups roughly chopped napa or Chinese cabbage
- 1/2 cup snow peas, trimmed
- 2 cups bean sprouts
- 1 bunch green onions, chopped (*including the white parts and some of the green*) **for garnish**
- canola oil cooking spray

1. Cut each pound of tofu into 8 equal triangles (*for a total of 16*) and marinate in 1 cup of Teriyaki Sauce. Set aside.

2. Trim and slice mushrooms and rinse them. (*The excess water on the mushrooms adds needed moisture during fat-free sautéing.*) Set aside.

3. Begin cooking the rice, following package directions. Spray a large sauté pan or griddle once with cooking spray and set over medium-high heat.

4. Add all the vegetables except the snow peas and bean sprouts to the pan. Add the ginger and garlic.

5. Sauté, stirring frequently, until the vegetables are just cooked and still crunchy, about 8 to 12 minutes.

6. Stir in about 1 tablespoon of Teriyaki Sauce and add bean sprouts and snow peas. Allow vegetables to cook while you sauté tofu.

7. Spray a second sauté pan once with cooking spray and add tofu triangles.

8. Sauté tofu about 2 minutes on each side.

9. In a pasta bowl or shallow soup plate, place 1/2 cup rice. Spoon 1/8 of the vegetable mix over the rice. Cover with 1 tablespoon of Teriyaki Sauce and 2 tofu triangles. Sprinkle with green onions and serve.

YIELD: 8 SERVINGS

Per serving, including Teriyaki Sauce: 327 Calories, 3.4g Fat, 0.5g Saturated Fat, 0g Cholesterol, 18.4g Protein, 62g Carbohydrate, 8.7g Fiber, 1316mg Sodium

TERIYAKI SAUCE

This sauce will keep in the refrigerator for about 8 days. It's great on steamed fish and grilled chicken.

- 1/2 cup honey
- 2 cups water
- 1 cup low-sodium soy sauce or low-sodium tamari soy sauce
- 2 tablespoons rice flour
- 1 teaspoon crushed garlic
- 1 teaspoon grated fresh ginger

1. Place all ingredients in a saucepan.

2. Bring to a boil and turn down to a simmer.

3. Cook, stirring occasionally, until thick enough to coat the back of a spoon, about 15 minutes.

YIELD: 3 CUPS

THREE-BEAN CHILI
(*photo on page 43*)

This dish can be made in advance and kept frozen up to 1 month until ready to use. If you want to make a spicier chili add 1 or more chopped jalapeño peppers while the chili is cooking. Begin preparing the beans the night before.

- ³/4 **cup dried black beans**
- ³/4 **cup dried pinto beans**
- ³/4 **cup dried kidney beans**
- 8 **cups water**
- 1 **pasilla or poblano chili**
- 2 **cups corn kernels, fresh or frozen** (*use a serrated knife to cut fresh kernels from cob; freeze stripped cobs for making corn broth*)
- 2 **cups carrots, peeled and diced**
- 1 **medium Roasted Onion, diced (about 1 cup; page 76)**
- 1 **tablespoon canned green chilies**
- 2 **14.5-ounce cans diced low-sodium tomatoes, including juice**
- 3 **cups water**
- 2 **tablespoons chili powder**
- 2 **teaspoons ground cumin**
- ¹/2 **cup mirin (sweetened Japanese rice wine), optional**
- 2 **tablespoons corn flour or whole wheat flour**
  ground black pepper to taste

- ¹/2 **teaspoon sea salt**
- 6 **fat-free tortillas, for garnish, optional**
- 6 **green onions, for garnish**

1. Pick over beans to remove pebbles and other debris. Combine beans in a large bowl and cover with 8 cups warm water. Leave overnight. (*This will reduce the gas-producing qualities of the beans by washing away some of the complex sugars and will speed up the cooking time.*) The next day, rinse the beans well. Place in a soup pot and cover with water. Bring to a low boil.

2. Cook until just soft, about 1 hour. Drain. Meanwhile, prepare the other ingredients.

3. Dice pasilla chili, making certain your fingers do not touch the seeds. (*If you have sensitive skin you may want to wear rubber gloves, since the chili oil can burn. Be especially careful not to touch your eyes after you have been handling chilies.*)

4. Place all ingredients, except flour, salt and garnishes in a large pot with the cooked beans.

5. Cook for 30 minutes on low heat, stirring occasionally. Meanwhile preheat oven to 350°.

6. Add flour and cook 5 minutes longer.

7. Season with salt.

8. To serve: toast tortillas in preheated oven until golden and crispy. Place tortilla on plate and ladle the chili over the tortilla. Sprinkle with diced green onions.

YIELD: 2¹/2 QUARTS (6 SERVINGS)

Per serving: 289 Calories, 1.9g Fat, 0.3g Saturated Fat, 0g Cholesterol, 13g Protein, 55g Carbohydrate, 14.2g Fiber, 318 mg Sodium

TOFU DOG CASSEROLE WITH A PRETZEL CRUST

This is an easy dish to prepare and makes a fun change from hot dogs on a bun. You can make the baked beans several days ahead (or even weeks ahead if you freeze them). To save time, buy ready-made fat-free vegetarian baked beans.

> 2 **medium potatoes, peeled and diced (about 2 cups)**
> 4 **large carrots, diced (about 2 cups)**
> 8 **fat-free tofu dogs**
> 6 **cups Baked Beans, prepared at least 1 day ahead (page 75) or 3 cans vegetarian baked beans**
> 6 **frozen fat-free pretzels**
>   **mustard in a squeeze bottle (garnish)**

1. Preheat oven to 350°.

2. Cook potatoes in boiling water until tender, but not mushy, about 20 minutes. Drain.

3. Blanch carrots in boiling water until just tender, about 6 minutes.

4. Cut each tofu dog into 5 pieces.

5. In a large bowl, toss together baked beans, tofu dogs, carrots and potatoes.

6. Divide mixture among 6 small casserole dishes. Cover each with a frozen pretzel.

7. Bake in preheated oven until pretzel is soft and slightly crunchy and filling is heated through, about 30 minutes.

8. Decorate the top of each casserole with mustard stripes or any other design you please, squeezed from a plastic bottle.

YIELD: **6 INDIVIDUAL CASSEROLES**

Per serving: 564 Calories, 1.6g Fat, 0.4g Saturated Fat, 0g Cholesterol, 37.4g Protein, 104g Carbohydrate, 16.9g Fiber, 1619mg Sodium

UNDERSTANDING MARKETING TERMS

"Lite," "Reduced Fat," "Natural," "Fat Free." What do these terms actually mean? Not necessarily what you might think.

The popular terms that frequently appear on a food's label are little more than a marketing device. Better to evaluate ingredient lists and nutrition facts than the manufacturer's claims on the packaging.

Here are some widely used terms:

Reduced or less fat: Has at least 25 percent less fat per serving than the "regular" full-fat food cited on the label. This product can still derive most of its calories from fat.

Lite or Light: Has at least 50 percent less fat or 1/3 fewer calories than the "regular" full-fat food. This product can still derive most of its calories from fat.

Low-fat: Has no more than 3 grams of fat per serving. This depends entirely on the quantity of a single serving.

Fat-free or nonfat: Less than one-half of 1 gram of fat per serving. Therefore, six servings of a "fat-free" product can contain nearly 3 grams of fat.

Reduced or Less Sodium: Has at least 25 percent less sodium per serving than the "regular" food cited on the label.

All Natural or Natural: Beware! This can mean anything, and thus it means nothing helpful. Even lard is all natural.

A tofu hot dog garnished with yellow mustard, sauerkraut and diced tomatoes is still one of Mike's favorite treats.

SOY AND SOYBEANS

Shiitake Miso Soup, page 22

TOFU. Tempeh. Miso. Natto. Yuba. The less-exotic-sounding lecithin, soy milk, soy flour and bean sprouts. In recent years, nutritionists and research scientists have been able to confirm what Asian families have known for 2,000 years: the soybean is the vegetable that most nearly provides the complete diet necessary for good health.

Soybeans are rich in vitamins and minerals and the usaturated fats that help the body break down cholesterol. Soybeans are high in B vitamins and have the same soluble fiber as oat bran. Soy protein is high in folic acid, lysine, iron, zinc and calcium. Specifically, soy protein contains genistein, a chemical that interferes with the reproduction of prostate cancer cells—and which, except for soy products, is largely absent from the American diet.

Soybeans and most soy products do contain a fair amount of fat, and for years Americans processed the bean to remove the fat, in order to use the resulting oil for cooking. What was left over was fed to livestock, lucky for them— they eat the most beneficial component of· the bean. It is the soy protein that contains the isoflavones, including genistein, that may inhibit prostate cancer progression.

In the human diet, substituting soy protein for animal proteins has many potential benefits, both by addition and subtraction. But soy foods such as tofu are not a reliable and precise source of soy protein, because they vary in the amount of isoflavones they contain, depending on how

Tempeh, used in the Vegetable Reuben, page 68, and with Baked Beans, page 75.

the soybean is grown and how the food is processed. The most efficient way to ensure that your body gets the most beneficial components of the soybean is to add at least 20 to 40 grams of soy protein isolate powder to your daily diet (recipes for shakes, page 84).

In those countries where soy is a staple of the diet—Japan, China, Taiwan and others—rates of many forms of cancer and heart disease are strikingly low. In Japan, for example, the rate of prostate cancer mortality among men is one-fifth of what it is in the United States. (Of course, these national diets benefit not just from the presence of soy protein but from the near-total absence of high-fat dairy products and a far lower consumption of meat. These diets also benefit from substantial quantities of fruits and vegetables.)

For thousands of years, soybeans have been part of the crop cycle in Asia. Only about 2,000 years ago, with the discovery of the process of fermentation, did soy became a staple of the human diet, mostly in pastes and sauces. Sometime after 200 B.C., the Chinese developed a way to mold soy products in blocks, and what we know as tofu became the primary source of protein in Asia.

BUT soy was unknown in the Americas until less than 200 years ago. As clipper ships raced back across the Pacific, carrying Chinese silks to America, their lower holds were packed with soybeans, simply to provide ballast. When the ships docked on America's West Coast, the beans were unceremoniously dumped ashore, and a few enterprising people picked them up and planted them.

From this humble arrival, the bean became a major source of cattle feed. The United States is now the leading grower of soybeans, producing more than half of the world's crop each year.

Along with the growing production has come widespread scientific research in the last few decades, and the benefits of adapting this cattle diet for humans are persuasive.

"My father had a stroke at age 38, and all his male relatives died of strokes in their 50s and 60s," said Dr. James W. Anderson, explaining his interest in finding ways to reduce cholesterol. Dr. Anderson led an analysis of 38 medical studies (published in the New England Journal of Medicine in 1995) that found that soy protein lowers low-density lipoproteins (the "bad" cholesterol) while leaving unaffected the high-density "good" lipoproteins. "Soy protein diets do not produce high cholesterol and atherosclerosis, like diets containing animal protein," Dr. Anderson said. Other research has shown that soy protein inhibits angiogenesis—the growth of blood vessels that nourish a tumor's growth.

THE recipes in this book provide many ways to add soy to your diet, and your imagination can guide you to even more. Soy flour can be used in baked goods, substituting for up to 20 percent of the total flour amount. Silken tofu can be substituted for yogurt or cream cheeses in some recipes. Soy milk can be poured onto breakfast cereal.

It's time to remove soy from the list of "exotic" or "ethnic" foods—and to experiment with more ways to bring it into your family's diet.

UNDERSTANDING TOFU

Three main types of tofu—firm, soft and silken—are widely available in stores, usually sold in water-filled tubs or vacuum packs that are displayed in the produce section (if tofu is not there, look in the dairy section of the store).

Firm tofu maintains its shape well in stir-fry dishes or soups. A 4-ounce serving typically contains 6 grams of fat.

Soft tofu works well in recipes that call for blending. A 4-ounce serving typically contains 5 grams of fat.

Silken tofu has a consistency like custard and works well in puréed or blended dishes. A 4-ounce serving typically has 2.4 grams of fat.

All tofu is low in saturated fat and contains no cholesterol. Lower-fat and reduced-fat tofu is also available. We recommend using the lowest-fat tofu you can find in whatever form the recipes call for.

Tofu should be kept cold, and once the package is open, tofu should be covered with fresh water for storage. It can be kept for up to a week, with the water changed daily. Tofu can also be frozen for up to five months. When defrosted, it will be caramel in color, with a spongy texture that soaks up marinades.

LASAGNE WITH "SOYSAGE"

over 60 minutes

This is a healthy remake of the classic dish. To prepare ahead, assemble the dish, wrap airtight and freeze for up to 1 month. When you're ready to use the dish, defrost or add 30 to 45 minutes to the cooking time and bake frozen.

- 1 recipe Fresh Pasta Sheets (page 51) or 1 pound of egg-free dry lasagne or egg-free no-boil lasagne
- 1 recipe Marinara Sauce (page 64)
- 1 pound fat-free vegetarian sausage , bulk or sliced links (preferably soy-based)
- 2 teaspoons crushed red pepper flakes
- 1 tablespoon fennel seeds or anise seeds, optional
- 1 pound or 1 block low-fat silken tofu (2 cups)
- 3/4 pound fat-free mozzarella-style soy cheese, grated by hand (about 1 1/2 cups)
- 1 tablespoon garlic powder or granulated garlic
- 3 tablespoons chopped fresh basil or 2 tablespoons dried
- 1/8 teaspoon sea salt

1. Preheat oven to 350°.

2. Prepare Marinara Sauce according to the recipe, with the following changes: Purée tomatoes before cooking them. Cook soy sausages along with onions and garlic. Add red pepper flakes and fennel or anise when you add the pureed tomatoes. (*The fennel or anise gives the sauce a stronger Italian-sausage taste.*)

3. Drain tofu and crush by hand. Add to a mixing bowl with basil, garlic and salt. Mix together.

4. Coat the bottom of a 13"x 9" baking dish with Marinara Sauce and line with a layer of pasta.

5. Cover the pasta with more sauce, then spread a layer of 1/2 of the tofu mixture. Sprinkle with 1/3 of the soy cheese.

6. Repeat the layers of pasta, sauce, tofu and cheese. Finish with a layer of pasta, sauce and cheese.

7. Cover with a piece of parchment or wax paper and then with a layer of foil. (*The parchment will prevent the soy cheese from sticking to the foil.*)

8. Bake in preheated oven for 40 minutes. Remove foil and parchment and bake until cheese is lightly browned, about 10 minutes.

9. To serve, ladle some sauce into a plate and place a portion of lasagne on it. Leftover Marinara Sauce may be frozen.

YIELD: 10 TO 12 SERVINGS.

Per serving: 380 Calories, 1.5g Fat, 0.1g Saturated Fat, 0g Cholesterol, 27.6g Protein, 55g Carbohydrate, 4g Fiber, 612mg Sodium

SPINACH CANNELLONI IN FRESH TOMATO SAUCE

You can use the crepe recipe from this dish to make Red Chili Crepes and Dessert Crepes. Add 1 ½ teaspoons chili powder to the crepe mix for red chili crepes or 1 ½ teaspoons vanilla extract for dessert crepes. I prefer to use all organic white flour rather than whole wheat for a fat-free crepe—it produces a much lighter result. Make these crepes in advance, if you like, wrap them well and freeze until needed. Vary the filling according to your own taste.

CREPES

- 2¼ cups plain 1% soy milk
- 1 cup plus 2 tablespoons all-purpose flour
- 1 cup plus 2 tablespoons nonfat egg substitute
- 4 tablespoons plus 2 teaspoons unsweetened applesauce
- ⅛ teaspoon sea salt
- canola oil cooking spray

SPINACH FILLING

- 1 medium onion, roasted (page 76) or raw
- 24 ounces raw spinach, rinsed, (about 6 quarts of spinach or use three 8-to 10-ounce boxes frozen spinach, thawed and squeezed dry)
- ½ cup brewer's yeast flakes
- ½ cup low-fat tofu (4 ounces)
- 2 egg whites
- 2 tablespoons granulated onion
- 1 teaspoon sea salt

TO MAKE CREPES

1. Place all ingredients in a blender or food processor and mix until smooth.

2. Pour batter into a bowl and allow to rest for 20 minutes.

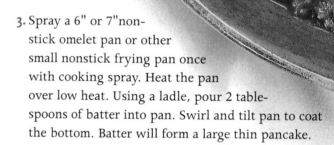

3. Spray a 6" or 7"nonstick omelet pan or other small nonstick frying pan once with cooking spray. Heat the pan over low heat. Using a ladle, pour 2 tablespoons of batter into pan. Swirl and tilt pan to coat the bottom. Batter will form a large thin pancake.

4. Cook over very low heat until mixture thickens and browns around the edges.

5. Flip the pancake with the tip of a paring knife or a small spatula and cook on reverse side for 2 minutes.

6. Flip crepe onto a clean platter and repeat process until batter is used up. If the pan heats up and crepes start cooking too fast, remove pan from heat to let it cool down.

7. To freeze crepes for use at a later time, layer cooled crepes between sheets of parchment paper, wrap the stack in plastic wrap and then in foil and freeze up to 1 month.

TO MAKE FILLING

1. If you're not using a roasted onion, peel and slice a raw onion. Spray a sauté pan once and add onion to the pan. Cook over low heat until onion is soft and light brown, about 10 minutes.

2. Blanch spinach in boiling water for 2 minutes. (*If using frozen spinach, skip this step.*) Strain.

3. Place all ingredients in a food processor and puree.

4. Scrape mixture into a bowl.

TO ASSEMBLE CANNELLONI

1. Preheat oven to 350°.

2. Place 2 or 3 tablespoons of filling in center of crepe. Roll up jelly-roll style.

3. Repeat with remaining crepes and filling.

4. Spread a thin layer of Fresh Tomato Sauce on the bottom of a 3-quart casserole dish. Place cannelloni on top of sauce. Cover cannelloni with the remaining sauce.

5. Cover pan with foil and bake in preheated oven until hot and bubbly, about 30 minutes.

YIELD: 6 SERVINGS (16-20 CANNELLONI)

Per serving, including Fresh Tomato Sauce: 336 Calories, 3.7g Fat, 0.9g Saturated Fat, 0g Cholesterol, 21.5g Protein, 62g Carbohydrate, 11.6g Fiber, 750mg Sodium

FRESH TOMATO SAUCE

This is a light sauce to serve over pasta, with Greek Spinach Pie (page 61) or with chicken or fish.

- **15** large vine-ripened tomatoes
- **3** tablespoons chopped fresh garlic
- **3** tablespoons chopped fresh basil or 2 teaspoons dried
- **⅛** teaspoon sea salt
- canola oil cooking spray

1. Bring a large pot of water to a boil.

2. Core tomatoes and cut an X on the bottom side with a paring knife.

3. Place tomatoes in boiling water for 1 to 2 minutes to loosen skin.

4. Remove to a bowl of cold water until they're cool enough to handle.

5. Peel tomatoes, cut in half and squeeze each over a bowl to remove seeds. Discard the seeds.

6. In batches, place tomatoes in a blender or food processor and purée.

7. Spray a large saucepan once with cooking spray and place over low heat.

8. Add chopped garlic to the pan and dried basil, if using, and cook for 1 minute.

9. Add puréed tomatoes and cook for 20 minutes, stirring occasionally.

10. Add fresh basil and salt when sauce has finished cooking.

YIELD: 6 CUPS

Per 1-cup serving: 103 Calories, 1.6g Fat, 0.2g Saturated Fat, 0g Cholesterol, 4.2g Protein, 23g Carbohydrate, 5.1g Fiber, 90mg Sodium

SPAGHETTI SQUASH MANICOTTI IN A THREE-HERB MARINARA SAUCE

Do-ahead tip: Bake the spaghetti squash the day before you make the dish.

- **1 large spaghetti squash**
- **1 recipe Pasta Dough (see right) or 12 ounces fresh pasta sheets**
- **½ recipe Marinara Sauce (page 64) or 1 quart commercial marinara sauce; add to either sauce:**
- **1 teaspoon fresh rosemary** (*if available*)
- **1 teaspoon fresh basil or ½ teaspoon dried pinch of crushed red pepper flakes.**
- **1-2 tablespoons chopped fresh basil**

1. Preheat oven to 350°. Bake the spaghetti squash 30 minutes. Pierce the squash and bake until soft, about 1 hour longer. Cool squash.

2. Cut open squash, scoop out seeds and discard. Scrape out spaghetti-like strands of squash with a fork. Put the squash in a bowl and add the fresh basil. Toss.

3. Place a pasta square on a work surface. Place a heaping tablespoon of spaghetti squash in the center of each square. Fold edges in and roll as you would an egg roll. Repeat with remaining ingredients.

4. Cover the bottom of a 15"x 10" baking dish with 1 cup of Marinara Sauce. Place stuffed manicotti over sauce and spoon 2 cups sauce over the pasta. Cover with foil and bake in preheated oven until pasta is soft and sauce is bubbling, about 45 minutes. Remove from oven and let rest for 10 minutes. Serve with additional sauce.

YIELD: **6 SERVINGS**

Per serving: 262 Calories, 1.3g Fat, 0.2g Saturated Fat, 0g Cholesterol, 10.5g Protein, 54g Carbohydrate, 7g Fiber, 368mg Sodium

PASTA DOUGH

Use this dough for manicotti, lasagne, ravioli, fettuccini or spaghetti. To vary the flavor, add 1 tablespoon of chopped fresh herbs, such as basil, rosemary or chives.

- **2 cups all-purpose flour**
- **¾ cup nonfat egg substitute**

1. Place ingredients in food processor and process until dough forms a ball.

2. Turn dough onto a floured surface and knead for 2 minutes. Flatten dough into a disk. Wrap in plastic wrap and let rest. Chill for 30 minutes.

3. To roll dough by hand, dust a work surface lightly with flour. Use a rolling pin to roll the dough as thin as possible. Lightly reflour the surface under the dough often and give the dough quarter turns to prevent sticking. Work the dough into a long rectangle ¼" thick.

4. If you're using a pasta machine, first roll the dough into a flat rectangle with a rolling pin. Then place through widest setting on machine. Repeat 5 times running it through progressively thinner settings.

5. Cut dough into 5"x 5" squares.

YIELD: **12 OUNCES OF PASTA**

NOT-MEAT LOAF WITH SHIITAKE MUSHROOM GRAVY

over 60 minutes

If possible, start this dish 2 days before you plan to serve it. That way you can cook the rice and lentils one day, assemble and bake the loaf the next day and let the finished loaf rest in the refrigerator for 24 hours, which will make it easier for you to cut neat, even slices. For a more attractive presentation, leave the loaf whole. Ideal accompaniments for this dish are Shiitake Mushroom Gravy, Mashed Potatoes (page 81) and a bouquet of freshly steamed vegetables.

- 2 cups mushrooms, trimmed
- 2 medium onions, sliced (about 2 cups)
- 2 cups cooked brown rice (made from 1 cup raw)
- 2 cups cooked lentils (made from 1 cup raw)
- 1 cup ketchup, divided
- 1/3 cup low-fat firm tofu (about 2 1/2 ounces)
- 1/3 cup low-sodium tamari soy sauce
- 2 tablespoons granulated onion
- 1 teaspoon granulated garlic
- 1/2 cup egg whites (about 5 or 6 large whites) or nonfat egg substitute
- 1 cup rolled oats
- 2 large carrots, grated (about 1 cup)
- 1/2 cup mashed potato flakes
- 1 tablespoon fresh thyme or 1/4 teaspoon dried thyme
- 1/2 teaspoon sea salt
  ground black pepper to taste
  canola oil cooking spray

1. Preheat oven to 350°.

2. Slice mushrooms and rinse them in a colander. (*The water will add needed moisture during the sautéing process.*)

3. Spray a large sauté pan once with cooking spray. Cook onions and mushrooms over low heat until the mushrooms soften, about 10 to 12 minutes.

4. Place mushroom and onion mixture in a food processor. Add rice, lentils, 3/4 cup ketchup, tofu, tamari sauce, granulated onion and garlic and process until smooth.

5. Add egg whites and process again.

6. Place mixture in a bowl and add oats, carrots, potato flakes and thyme. Mix well.

7. If you are planning to unmold the loaf, line the bottom of a 9"x5"x3" loaf pan with parchment paper that has been cut to fit. Spray sides of pan with cooking spray. If you are not going to unmold the loaf, omit the parchment paper.

8. Place mixture in pan and spread evenly.

9. Use a knife to make an X-shaped groove in the top of the loaf.

10. Spread remaining 1/4 cup ketchup over the top.

11. Bake in preheated oven until firm to the touch, about 1 1/2 hours.

12. To unmold: allow the loaf to cool to room temperature, then invert it on a plate or board and remove parchment paper. Cover the bottom with another plate or board and turn the loaf over so that it is right side up. Slice and place slices on sprayed baking sheet. Cover with foil to reheat at 350° until heated through, about 15 minutes. If you are not unmolding the loaf, slice it in the pan.

13. Serve with Shiitake Mushroom Gravy. (*Save leftovers for sandwiches.*)

YIELD: 8 SERVINGS.

Per serving: 262 Calories, 1.8g Fat, 0.3g Saturated Fat, 0g Cholesterol, 13.2g Protein, 50g Carbohydrate, 8.2g Fiber, 996mg Sodium

SHIITAKE MUSHROOM GRAVY

This gravy is also great on pasta and mashed potatoes.

- 1 medium onion, sliced (about 1 cup)
- 1 cup shiitake mushrooms, trimmed and sliced
- 3½ cups water
- ¼ cup low-sodium tamari soy sauce
- ¼ cup plus 1 tablespoon rice flour
- 1 tablespoon fresh thyme or ¼ teaspoon dried thyme
- 2 teaspoons fresh sage or ⅛ teaspoon dried sage
- 1 tablespoon lavender, optional
  canola oil cooking spray

1. Spray a medium saucepan once with cooking spray.

2. Place over low heat and add onions and mushrooms.

3. Cover and cook vegetables until they begin to exude moisture, about 10 minutes, stirring occasionally.

4. Add water and tamari sauce and cook for 10 minutes.

5. Add flour, stirring with a whisk to eliminate lumps.

6. Simmer 10 minutes, stirring occasionally.

7. Pour gravy through a fine strainer into a clean saucepan to remove mushrooms and onions, or leave it unstrained for a rough, country-style gravy.

8. Add herbs, heat and serve.

YIELD: 3 CUPS UNSTRAINED OR 2¼ CUPS STRAINED

Per 2-tablespoon serving: 9 Calories, 0.1g Fat, 0g Saturated Fat, 0g Cholesterol, 0.2g Protein, 2g Carbohydrate, 0.2g Fiber, 0 mg Sodium

VEGETABLE FRITTATA WITH ROASTED TOMATO SALSA

Serve this dish with a baby green salad dressed with Raspberry Vinaigrette (page 35). Shred soy cheese by hand. Fat-free soy cheese is too rubbery for the food processor; it can crack the work bowl. (I've seen it happen—twice!)

FRITTATA

- 1 pound mushrooms, trimmed and sliced
- 1 large onion, peeled, halved and sliced thin
- 1 large red pepper, diced
- 2 pounds or 2 blocks low-fat tofu (4 cups)
- 1 cup egg whites (about 10 to 12 large whites) or nonfat egg substitute
- ¼ cup umeboshi plum vinegar or ½ to ¾ teaspoon sea salt
- 3 tablespoons chopped fresh basil or 1 tablespoon dried basil
- 1 tablespoon plus 1 teaspoon granulated onion
- 4 medium zucchini, shredded
- 12 ounces fat-free soy cheese, grated by hand (about 1½ cups)
  canola oil cooking spray

ROASTED TOMATO SALSA

- 4 large vine-ripened tomatoes, cored
- 1 large onion, peeled
- 2 shallots, peeled (about 2 tablespoons chopped)
- ¼ teaspoon sea salt
- ¼ cup chopped fresh chives
  canola oil cooking spray

TO MAKE THE FRITTATA:

1. Preheat oven to 350°.

2. Rinse sliced mushrooms in a colander to remove any dirt.

(*Washing the mushrooms after they're sliced adds moisture needed during the sautéing process in fat-free cooking.*)

3. Spray a heavy sauté pan once with cooking spray. Place over low heat. Add onion and pepper and cook for 2 minutes, stirring constantly.

4. Add mushrooms and cook until they soften, about 5 minutes. Remove from heat to cool.

5. In a food processor fitted with a chopping blade, process tofu until smooth. Add egg whites, vinegar, basil and granulated onion.

6. Combine mushroom mixture, tofu mixture, zucchini and soy cheese in a large bowl. Mix lightly using rubber spatula.

7. Lightly coat the inside of a 9" deep-dish quiche pan with cooking spray. Spread mixture in prepared pan.

8. Bake in preheated oven until frittata is firm and the top is light gold, about 1½ hours.

9. Slice into 8 pieces using a serrated knife and serve immediately with Roasted Tomato Salsa.

YIELD: 8 SERVINGS

TO MAKE THE SALSA:

1. Preheat oven to 350°. Spray a baking sheet once with cooking spray.

2. Place tomatoes, onion and shallots on baking sheet and bake until skins brown and blister, about 45 minutes.

3. Put roasted vegetables and salt in a blender or food processor. Purée.

4. Just before serving, pour sauce into a sauté pan and heat until simmering. Pour into a serving bowl, sprinkle with chives and serve with frittata.

YIELD: 2 CUPS

Per serving: 184 Calories, 2.1g Fat, 0.3g Saturated Fat, 0g Cholesterol, 23.4g Protein, 20g Carbohydrate, 4.8g Fiber, 585mg Sodium

CHILES RELLENOS IN A TOMATO JALAPEÑO BROTH

The versatile corn filling in this recipe can be the basis for a variety of dishes. For Tortillas Rellenas, take a corn tortilla, dip it in egg white, sauté it in a nonstick pan, fill it with corn filling, warm under the broiler, roll it like an omelet and serve it with Ranchero Sauce (page 58). Or, if you prefer, add 1 teaspoon of chili powder to Crepe recipe (page 48), fill crepes with corn mixture and serve with Ranchero Sauce for Southwestern Corn Crepes. To make Corn Cakes, add 2 tablespoons of ground tortilla crumbs to filling mixture, form patties, lightly dust patties with flour, sauté on both sides in a lightly sprayed pan and finish cooking in a 350° oven for about 20 minutes. Serve these Corn Cakes with Pea-camole (page 71). The Tomato Jalapeño Broth is a light Mexican sauce. Try stuffing cabbage with the taco salad "meat" mix (page 26) and cover it with this sauce for a Southwestern Stuffed Cabbage.

CHILES RELLENOS

- **1 medium onion, sliced** (about 1 cup)
- **1 red pepper, sliced** (about 1 cup)
- **2 cups fresh or frozen corn kernels** (*use a serrated knife to cut fresh kernels from cob; freeze stripped cobs for making Corn Broth, page 16*)

¼ cup plus 2 tablespoons low-fat silken tofu (6 ounces)

1 teaspoon ground cumin

⅛ teaspoon sea salt

ground black pepper to taste

2 tablespoons chopped cilantro

12 pasilla or poblano chilies

1 cup egg whites (about 10-12 large whites)

1 cup cornmeal

canola oil cooking spray

JALAPEÑO TOMATO BROTH

2 pounds fresh tomatoes (5 or 6 medium), quartered

1 small onion, peeled and quartered

½-1 small jalapeño pepper, split and stem removed

1½ cups water

⅛ teaspoon sea salt

TO MAKE CHILES RELLENOS

1. Spray a sauté pan once with cooking spray and place over low heat. Add onion and pepper and cook, stirring occasionally, for 5 minutes.

2. Add corn kernels, stir mixture, cover and cook 5 minutes, shaking the pan occasionally.

3. Place cooked vegetables, tofu, cumin, salt and pepper in a food processor fitted with a metal blade and process.

4. Transfer to mixing bowl and stir in cilantro. Set aside.

5. Roast chilies on a grill, under the broiler or directly over the flame of a stove burner. Turn and continue to roast until all sides are blackened. Transfer to a bowl and cover the bowl with plastic wrap to allow the chilies to steam at least 20 minutes, which will loosen their skins.

6. To peel peppers: Hold peppers one at a time under slow-running cold water and gently peel off skin leaving the stem intact. Slit the pepper and gently rinse out the seeds.

7. Stuff pepper with 2 to 3 tablespoons of corn filling.

8. Preheat oven to 350°.

9. Place egg whites in the bowl of an electric mixer and whip until soft peaks form. (*Do not over-whip or the whites will not stick to the chili.*) Pour cornmeal into a second bowl. Roll stuffed chili in cornmeal and then in egg whites.

10. Spray a nonstick sauté pan once with cooking spray. Sauté chili on both sides until light brown. Transfer chili to a baking sheet that has been sprayed once with cooking spray.

11. Finish cooking chilies in preheated oven. Bake until egg whites are light brown and filling is heated through, about 10 minutes. Serve two chilies in a pool of Jalapeño Tomato Broth.

YIELD: 6 SERVINGS

Per serving: 181 Calories, 1.2g Fat, 0.2g Saturated Fat, 0g Cholesterol, 9.7g Protein, 35g Carbohydrate, 4.1g Fiber, 150mg Sodium

TO MAKE JALAPEÑO TOMATO BROTH

1. Place tomatoes, onion, jalapeño and water in a large saucepan.

2. Place pan over high heat and bring to a boil. Turn down to a simmer and cover pot. Cook until tomatoes are tender, about 20 minutes.

3. Purée sauce in a blender or a food processor fitted with a metal blade.

4. Transfer to a clean pan and season with salt. Warm broth before serving.

YIELD: 1 QUART

Per 2-tablespoon serving: 14 Calories, 0.2g Fat, 0g Saturated Fat, 0g Cholesterol, 0.6g Protein, 3g Carbohydrate, 0.5g Fiber, 23mg Sodium

ENCHILADA PIE WITH RANCHERO SAUCE

To make a Tortilla Pie, substitute fat-free flour tortillas for corn tortillas, black beans for pinto beans and add 1 cup diced zucchini. You can turn up the heat by adding sliced roasted jalapeño peppers to the Ranchero Sauce.

ENCHILADA PIE

6	ears corn
4	cups cooked pinto beans (1½ cups dried)
½ to 1	cup chopped cilantro
½	cup chopped green onions (*use the white part and some of the green*)
1 to 2	teaspoons ground cumin
1	recipe Ranchero Sauce (see below)
20	corn tortillas made with no added fat
1	pound fat-free jack-style soy cheese, grated by hand (about 2 cups)
⅛	teaspoon sea salt
	ground black pepper to taste

RANCHERO SAUCE

6	cups Vegetable Stock (page 18)
4	medium onions, sliced thin (about 4 cups)
2	large red peppers, cut into strips (about 2 cups)
2	large green peppers, cut into strips (about 2 cups)
1	28-ounce can tomato purée
1	14-ounce can diced low-sodium tomatoes, including juice
⅛	teaspoon sea salt
	ground black pepper to taste

TO MAKE ENCHILADA PIE

1. Preheat oven to 350°. Set a large pot of water over high heat and bring to a boil.

2. Blanch corn in boiling water for 2 minutes. Strip kernels from cob with a serrated knife.

3. In a large mixing bowl, combine corn, beans, cilantro, green onions and cumin.

4. Cover the bottom of a deep 12" round baking pan with a thin layer of Ranchero Sauce.

5. Spread 5 tortillas on top of the sauce, to cover the bottom of the pan. Spread Ranchero Sauce over the tortillas

6. Spread ⅓ of the bean mixture on top of the tortillas and sprinkle with ¼ of the grated cheese. Repeat layers of tortillas, bean mixture and cheese 2 more times.

7. Place the remaining 5 tortillas on top. Cover with Ranchero Sauce and sprinkle on remaining soy cheese.

8. Cover pan with parchment paper and then with foil. (*The parchment prevents the soy cheese from sticking.*)

9. Bake in preheated oven until cheese is melted and pie is steaming, about 40 minutes. Remove from oven and cut into serving pieces.

10. Ladle some Ranchero Sauce onto a plate. Serve a portion of pie onto the sauce.

YIELD: 8 TO 10 SERVINGS

Per serving: 590 Calories, 2.9g Fat, 0.4g Saturated Fat, 0g Cholesterol, 33.2g Protein, 117g Carbohydrate, 19.3g Fiber, 1120mg Sodium

TO MAKE RANCHERO SAUCE

1. Place all ingredients in a large saucepan over medium-high heat.

2. Bring to a boil and turn down to a simmer. Cook until peppers and onions are tender, about 25 minutes.

YIELD: 2½ QUARTS

Per 2-tablespoon serving: 17 Calories, 0.1g Fat, 0g Saturated Fat, 0g Cholesterol, 0.5g Protein, 4g Carbohydrate, 0.6g Fiber, 48mg Sodium

HOW TO MAKE SENSE OF A LABEL

Serving size: A quantity (such as 11 chips), a weight (1 oz.) or a volume (1 cup). In this box of snack crackers, a serving is 15 crackers.

Servings per container: A quick look at this number will provide an idea of whether the designated serving size is enough to satisfy you. This box contains "about 12" servings of crackers. Many people would easily consume a quarter of a box—at least three servings.

Calories: Number of calories in the listed serving size. In this box, a serving contains 140 calories.

Total Fat: Number of fat grams per serving. Each serving of these crackers has 4.5 grams of fat. Each gram of fat contains 9 calories. If you are attempting to limit fat content to the recommended 15 percent of your daily diet, a single serving of 15 crackers uses up 13 percent of the entire day's allowance of fat, based on a diet of 2,000 calories a day.

Cholesterol: Milligrams per serving.

Sodium: Milligrams per serving.

Total Carbohydrate: The combined total of three types of carbohydrates: dietary fiber, simple sugars and complex carbohydrates.

Sugars: Number of grams of simple sugars per serving. In this example, less than 1 of the 20 grams of carbohydrate come from simple sugars (sucrose, fructose, honey). The idea is to fill your diet with calories that come from complex carbohydrates and protein.

Vitamins and minerals: listed as percentages based on the Recommended Daily Allowances.

Calories from Fat: Of the number of calories in the serving, how many come from fat. If you are trying to limit your fat intake to no more than 15 percent of your daily calories, you would have to balance higher-fat foods like this with foods that had nearly no fat.

The Percent Daily Value column lists percentages based on the Agriculture Department's recommended diet of 30 percent of calories from fat. The guidelines envision a diet of 2,000 calories a day, with no more than 600 from fat. CaP CURE recommends that you consume no more than 15 percent of your calories from fat, or no more than 300 calories a day out of 2,000.

Saturated Fat: Of the total fat grams, this is the amount of saturated fat, a category that is listed separately because saturated fats are thought to increase the risk of heart disease. This listing does not include trans-hydrogenated fatty acids, which are polyunsaturated fats that have been chemically altered to have a longer shelf life. These trans-hydrogenated fats have been shown to increase cholesterol levels. These fats can be identified in the ingredient section of the food label as "partially hydrogenated oil."

Dietary Fiber: Grams per serving. The recommended amount of fiber per day is 25 to 35 grams. One serving of these crackers contains less than 1 gram.

Protein: Grams per serving.

This section lists Ingredients in descending order of quantity: The first ingredient here is enriched flour, the source of most of the complex carbohydrates. Skim-milk cheese is next, which is the product's main source of protein and calcium. Next is vegetable shortening, made from partially hydrogenated oils and the source of most of the product's fat.

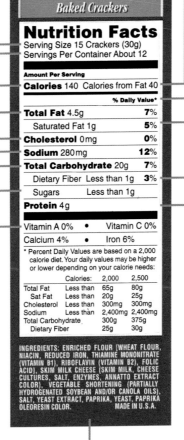

REDUCED FAT
Baked Crackers

Nutrition Facts
Serving Size 15 Crackers (30g)
Servings Per Container About 12

Amount Per Serving

Calories 140 Calories from Fat 40

% Daily Value*

Total Fat 4.5g	7%
Saturated Fat 1g	5%
Cholesterol 0mg	0%
Sodium 280mg	12%
Total Carbohydrate 20g	7%
Dietary Fiber Less than 1g	3%
Sugars Less than 1g	
Protein 4g	

Vitamin A 0%	•	Vitamin C 0%	
Calcium 4%	•	Iron 6%	

* Percent Daily Values are based on a 2,000 calorie diet. Your daily values may be higher or lower depending on your calorie needs:

		Calories:	2,000	2,500
Total Fat	Less than		65g	80g
Sat Fat	Less than		20g	25g
Cholesterol	Less than		300mg	300mg
Sodium	Less than		2,400mg	2,400mg
Total Carbohydrate			300g	375g
Dietary Fiber			25g	30g

INGREDIENTS: ENRICHED FLOUR [WHEAT FLOUR, NIACIN, REDUCED IRON, THIAMINE MONONITRATE (VITAMIN B1), RIBOFLAVIN (VITAMIN B2), FOLIC ACID], SKIM MILK CHEESE (SKIM MILK, CHEESE CULTURES, SALT, ENZYMES, ANNATTO EXTRACT COLOR), VEGETABLE SHORTENING (PARTIALLY HYDROGENATED SOYBEAN AND/OR CANOLA OILS), SALT, YEAST EXTRACT, PAPRIKA, YEAST, PAPRIKA OLEORESIN COLOR.   MADE IN U.S.A.

GREEK SPINACH PIE IN A PHYLLO NEST

This is a healthy remake of spanakopita, the classic Greek spinach pie. This mixture can also be used to make individual spinach rolls: Cut a phyllo sheet into 5 even strips. Place a tablespoon of filling in a corner of each strip, fold the corner over and continue to fold it in on itself, keeping a triangle shape, like folding a flag. Either version of the dish will freeze well up to 1 month if it is wrapped airtight. To make 1 large Spinach Pie, line a sprayed 15"x 10" baking dish with 3 sheets of phyllo, spread filling over phyllo and cover filling with another 3 sheets. Serving suggestion: Make Fresh Tomato Sauce (page 49) to serve alongside spinach pie.

- 1 **medium onion, roasted (page 76) or raw**
- 2½ **pounds raw spinach, rinsed (about 7 cups of spinach) or three 8- to 10-ounce boxes frozen spinach, thawed and squeezed dry**
- 12 **egg whites**
- ¾ **cup low-fat tofu (6 ounces)**
- 2 **tablespoons brewer's yeast**
- 1 **tablespoon granulated onion**
- 1 **tablespoon granulated garlic**
- ⅛ **teaspoon sea salt**
  ground black pepper to taste
- 12 **ounces fat-free mozzarella-style soy cheese, grated by hand (about 1½ cups)**
- ½ **pound phyllo dough at room temperature (12 sheets)**
- 1 **egg white, lightly beaten, for glazing pie**
  canola oil cooking spray

1. Preheat oven to 350°.

2. If you are not using a roasted onion, peel and slice raw onion. Spray a sauté pan once with cooking spray and cook onion over low heat until it is soft and light brown, about 10 minutes.

3. Blanch spinach in boiling water for 2 minutes. Remove spinach and drain. (*If using frozen spinach, skip this step.*)

4. Place all ingredients except cheese and phyllo in the work bowl of a food processor. Process until smooth.

5. Scrape spinach mixture into a bowl and add cheese.

6. Unroll phyllo and cover with a dry towel. Place a damp towel over the dry one. Keep stack of dough covered while you are working.

7. Spray the cups of a large capacity (1-cup) muffin tin with cooking spray. (*You will be making 8 individual spinach pies. If you don't have 2 muffin pans, you can do this in 2 batches of 4 spinach pies. Use the 4 corner muffin cups.*)

8. Remove 3 sheets of dough and cut in half to make 2 stacks of 8"x 12" rectangles. Line sprayed muffin cups with 3-layer stacks of phyllo. Repeat 3 more times to make a total of 8 3-sheet stacks. (*If you are using one 6-muffin pan, just prepare enough phyllo to line 4 cups. Leave the rest of the dough covered until you are ready to make the last 4 pies.*)

9. Spread ⅛ of the spinach mixture in each prepared muffin cup, about ¾ cup of filling.

10. Bring edges of phyllo together over the filling and gently twist to seal the tops of the pies.

11. Brush surface of phyllo with egg whites.

12. Bake in preheated oven until golden and firm, about 45 minutes.

YIELD: **8 SERVINGS**

Per serving: 213 Calories,
0.8g Fat, 0.1g Saturated Fat,
0g Cholesterol,
21.7g Protein,
29g Carbohydrate,
2.7g Fiber,
634 mg Sodium

HOMEMADE VEGETABLE PIZZA

I often make this pizza without cheese. It has a great flavor and cutting out the cheese will bring the sodium count way down. Do-ahead note: Make the dough up to 2 days in advance and refrigerate it or weeks ahead and freeze it.

PIZZA DOUGH

- 2 packets active dry yeast
- 1 cup warm water
  (*it should feel comfortably warm—not hot—to the touch*)
- 1 teaspoon honey
- 2½ cups all-purpose flour (or 1¾ cup all-purpose flour and ¼ cup whole wheat flour)
- ¾ teaspoon sea salt
- 2 teaspoons fresh rosemary, optional
- canola oil cooking spray
- cornmeal (*if you are baking the pie on a pizza stone*)

PIZZA SAUCE

- 1 tablespoon crushed fresh garlic
- 1 cup tomato purée
- 1 tablespoon tomato paste
- 2 teaspoons dried oregano
- 1 teaspoon dried basil
- ¼ teaspoon sea salt
- ¼ teaspoon crushed red pepper flakes, optional
- canola oil cooking spray

TOPPING

- 1 cup broccoli florets, blanched for 2 minutes in boiling water.
- 1 medium eggplant, sliced in ¼" rounds
- 2 cups mushrooms, trimmed
- 1 Roasted Onion, sliced into thin strips (page 76)
- 1 Roasted Red Pepper, peeled and cut into thin strips (page 20)
- 4 plum tomatoes, sliced lengthwise into thin slices
- ½ cup sun dried tomatoes (*not packed in oil*), **optional**
- 2 tablespoons chopped fresh basil (*if available*)
- ½ pound fat-free mozzarella-style soy cheese, grated by hand (about 1 cup)
- canola oil cooking spray

TO MAKE PIZZA DOUGH

1. In a small mixing bowl, soften yeast in warm water for 10 minutes. Stir in honey.

2. Fit a food processor with a dough blade. Add flour and salt to work bowl and pour in yeast mixture. Add optional rosemary.

3. Mix until dough forms a ball. Remove from bowl and knead on a floured surface for about 3 minutes.

4. Spray a mixing bowl with cooking spray. Place dough in bowl, turning once. Cover with a clean, dry towel. Put bowl in a warm place and allow to rise for 1 hour.

5. Turn dough out onto lightly floured board. Punch down dough to deflate it.

6. If making individual pizzas, cut dough into 6 equal parts and form into balls; otherwise shape into 1 large ball.

7. Spray a baking sheet once with cooking spray. Place dough on baking sheet and refrigerate at least 30 minutes.

8. Allow dough to return to room temperature before rolling.

TO MAKE SAUCE

1. Spray a saucepan once with cooking spray. Place over low heat. Add chopped garlic and cook for 2 minutes, stirring constantly.

2. Add tomato purée, paste, oregano, basil and red pepper flakes. Simmer for 15 minutes. Season with salt.

TO MAKE TOPPING

1. Spray a sauté pan once and place over low heat. Add eggplant rounds and lightly brown on both sides. Remove from pan and spray pan again.

2. Slice mushrooms and rinse well in a colander. Add to sauté pan and cook for 2 minutes. Remove from heat.

3. Place sun dried tomatoes in a small saucepan with water to cover. Bring to a boil and cook for 2 minutes, until soft. Drain and cut into thin strips.

TO ASSEMBLE THE PIZZA

1. Preheat oven to 450°. If you have a pizza stone, place it in the oven to heat.

2. Place room temperature dough on a floured surface and roll into a circle $\frac{1}{4}$ to $\frac{1}{8}$" thick.

3. Mold the crust edge with fingers so that it is slightly raised. If making individual pizzas, repeat for each dough ball.

4. Spray a baking sheet once with cooking spray. Place dough on sheet. (*If using pizza stone, sprinkle cornmeal on a pizza peel or on an upside-down, flat-bottomed baking sheet. Spread dough over cornmeal.*)

5. Pour sauce on dough. For large pizza use 1 cup of sauce. For small pizza use about $2\frac{1}{2}$ tablespoons each.

6. Put cheese over sauce (*Divide it evenly for individual pizzas.*)

7. Scatter vegetables over cheese. (*The vegetable covering will help the fat-free cheese to melt.*)

8. Bake in preheated oven until cheese melts, crust is hard, and vegetables are hot, about 20 minutes. (*Dough will not color very much, due to the absence of oil.*)

YIELD: 6 INDIVIDUAL PIZZAS OR 1 LARGE PIZZA (6 SERVINGS)

Per $\frac{1}{6}$ pizza serving: 340 Calories, 1.6g Fat, 0.2g Saturated Fat, 0g Cholesterol, 15g Protein, 64g Carbohydrate, 7.4g Fiber, 914mg Sodium

EGGPLANT PARMESAN STRUDEL WITH MARINARA SAUCE

This is a quick and easy recipe that looks and tastes as if it took hours to prepare. You can make the sauce days in advance or make a double batch and freeze half. The sauce is also good on any dish calling for meatless tomato sauce. To save time, you can use a good quality, commercial, fat-free marinara sauce. If your phyllo dough is frozen, thaw it overnight in the refrigerator. Remove it from the refrigerator 2 hours before you begin this dish—but keep it sealed against the air until the last minute.

2 medium eggplants, trimmed and cut into $\frac{1}{4}$" rounds

6 sheets of phyllo dough (whole wheat, if possible), at room temperature.

ground black pepper to taste, optional

2$\frac{1}{2}$ cups Marinara Sauce, divided (see below)

8 ounces fat-free mozzarella-style soy cheese, grated by hand (about 1 cup)

1 egg white, lightly beaten

canola oil cooking spray

1-2 tablespoons fat-free bread crumbs

1. Preheat oven to 350°. Line a baking sheet with parchment paper or lightly spray a baking sheet with cooking spray.

2. Spray a sauté pan or griddle lightly with cooking spray. Place over low heat. If you have a cast iron skillet, omit the cooking spray.

3. Lightly brown eggplant slices on both sides.

4. Transfer browned eggplant to a large mixing bowl and cover with plastic wrap to "steam" while you finish cooking the remaining eggplant.

5. Unroll phyllo and cover with a dry towel. Place a damp towel over the dry one. Keep stack of dough covered while you are working so that it doesn't dry out.

6. Stack 3 sheets of phyllo on a work surface. Brush the top layer lightly with egg white. Repeat, to make 6 layers of phyllo.

7. Place a double layer of eggplant across the narrow end of the dough, 3" in from the edge and from each side. Sprinkle with black pepper, if desired.

8. Spoon $\frac{1}{2}$ cup Marinara Sauce over the eggplant. Top with the cheese. Layer the remaining eggplant over the cheese.

9. Fold sides in. Then roll up, as if making a giant egg roll.

10. Place seam-side down on prepared baking sheet. Glaze the top with beaten egg white and dust with bread crumbs.

11. Bake in preheated oven until golden brown, about 30 minutes. Remove from oven and allow to rest 5 to 10 minutes before slicing. Cut into 6 equal portions.

12. Heat remaining Marinara Sauce in a small saucepan. Spoon some sauce onto a plate and place a slice of the strudel on top. Serve.

YIELD: 6 SERVINGS

Per serving: 212 Calories, 0.7g Fat, 0.1g Saturated Fat, 0g Cholesterol, 14.7g Protein 37g Carbohydrate, 0.7g Fiber, 416mg Sodium

MARINARA SAUCE

2 medium onions, chopped

$\frac{1}{4}$ cup fresh minced garlic (about 12 cloves)

2 29-ounce cans low-sodium diced tomatoes, including juice

1 28-ounce can low-sodium tomato purée

1 big handful fresh basil or $\frac{1}{4}$ cup dried basil

2 tablespoons dried oregano

$\frac{1}{8}$ teaspoon sea salt

ground black pepper to taste

canola oil cooking spray

1. Lightly spray a large saucepan or Dutch oven with cooking spray. Add onions and cook over low heat, stirring occasionally, until soft, about 5 minutes.

2. Add garlic and cook, stirring, for 1 minute.

3. Add tomatoes, purée, dried basil, oregano, salt and pepper.

4. Bring sauce to a simmer. Continue to simmer over low heat, stirring occasionally, until tomatoes have dissolved into a thick sauce, about 30 to 45 minutes.

5. If using fresh basil, add it at the end of cooking time.

YIELD: 2 QUARTS

Per 1-cup serving: 98.3 Calories, 0.2g Fat, 0.1g Saturated Fat, 0g Cholesterol, 3.9g Protein, 20.2g Carbohydrate, 6.2g Fiber, 88mg Sodium

GRANNY G'S SWEET AND SOUR STUFFED CABBAGE

over 60 minutes

This is a low-fat remake of my grandmother's traditional stuffed cabbage recipe.

- ½ cup raw brown basmati rice (2¼ cups cooked)
- 1¼ cups water
- 18 large leaves green cabbage (*Savoy works best*)
- 1 large onion, small diced (about 1 cup)
- 2 cloves garlic, crushed (about 1 teaspoon)
- 1 teaspoon dried oregano
- 2 cups vegetarian "meat"
  (such as fat-free burgers or ground soy meat)
- 1 cup fat-free vegetarian sausage
- 1 teaspoon granulated onion
- 1 teaspoon granulated garlic
- 1 14-ounce can diced low-sodium tomatoes, including juice
- ⅛ teaspoon sea salt
  ground black pepper to taste

  canola oil cooking spray
- 1 recipe Fresh Tomato Sauce (page 49) to which you have added ¾ teaspoon lemon juice, ¾ teaspoon grated lemon zest and ¾ teaspoon fruit sweetener or natural cane sugar

1. Put brown rice and water in a small saucepan. Bring to a boil over medium-high heat, turn down to a simmer and cover pot. Cook until rice has absorbed all the water, 25 to 45 minutes.

2. Set a pot of water over high heat and bring to a boil. Blanch cabbage leaves in boiling water for 30 seconds, until cabbage leaves are limp enough to roll. Drain and cool.

3. Preheat oven to 350°. Lightly spray a sauté pan with cooking spray. Set pan over low heat and add diced onion, garlic and oregano. Cook, stirring constantly, until onions are soft, about 5 minutes.

4. Add soy "meat" and sausage to pan and crumble with the back of a spoon. Add granulated onion and garlic and continue to cook until "meat" is warm, about 4 minutes.

5. Add tomatoes. Mix well and cook for another minute. Remove from heat.

6. Add cooked rice to "meat" mixture, season with salt and black pepper. Mix well.

7. Open cabbage leaves and place about 3 tablespoons of filling in the center of each. Roll up leaf, folding in sides and enclosing filling, as you would an egg roll.

8. Cover the bottom of a 15" x 10" baking dish with 2 cups Fresh Tomato Sauce. Arrange cabbage rolls on sauce and cover with about 3 cups more sauce. Cover pan with foil and bake in preheated oven until sauce is bubbling, about 30 to 40 minutes.

YIELD: 9 SERVINGS

Per serving: 139 Calories, 1.5g Fat, 0.2g Saturated Fat, 0g Cholesterol, 4.8g Protein, 30g Carbohydrate, 5.7g Fiber, 102mg Sodium

sandw
AND sandwiches

might be

HEARTY

or LIGHT

imaginative or classic.

They are certain to be delicious.

VEGETABLE REUBEN

Some people like this sandwich with a tablespoon of yellow mustard in addition to the traditional Thousand Island Dressing. For an old-fashioned deli experience, serve with sides of French Fries (next page), Coleslaw (see right) and a pickle. To reduce sodium, substitute white turkey meat for tempeh bacon.

- 16 tempeh bacon strips
- 8 slices fat-free rye or sourdough bread
- 8 ounces fat-free mozzarella-style soy cheese, sliced thin (about 1 cup)
- 1 cup Thousand Island Dressing (page 35)
- 1⅓ cups sauerkraut, drained
  canola oil cooking spray

1. Preheat oven to 350°. Line a baking sheet with parchment paper or spray once with cooking spray.

2. Place tempeh strips on prepared baking sheet. Bake in preheated oven until crispy, about 20 minutes. Remove from oven and set aside.

3. Spread out 4 slices of bread. On each slice, place 2 pieces of tempeh, ⅛ of the cheese, ¼ cup dressing, ⅓ cup sauerkraut, ⅛ of cheese and then 2 more pieces of tempeh.

4. Top each sandwich with a second slice of bread.

5. Spray a baking sheet once with cooking spray. Place sandwiches on prepared sheet and bake in preheated oven until cheese is melted and bread is toasted, about 20 minutes. Slice sandwiches in half and serve.

YIELD: 4 SANDWICHES

Per serving: 382 Calories, 5.4g Fat, 1.2g Saturated Fat, 0g Cholesterol, 31.5g Protein, 50g Carbohydrate, 7.2g Fiber, 1586mg Sodium

COLESLAW

- ½ head green cabbage
- ½ head red cabbage
- 2 large carrots, peeled
- ½ cup water
- ⅓ cup low-fat silken tofu (about 2½ ounces)
- 3 tablespoons maple or natural cane sugar
- 3 tablespoons granulated onion
- 2 shallots, peeled (to equal about 2 tablespoons chopped)
- 2 tablespoons brown rice vinegar (you may substitute white)
- 2 teaspoons Dijon mustard
- ⅛ teaspoon sea salt
  ground black pepper to taste
- ¼ teaspoon celery seed

1. Shred red and green cabbage. (You can use the shredding blade of a food processor; however, I find that cutting the cabbage in thin shreds with a sharp knife gives a better appearance—a method called "chiffonade.") Transfer to a large bowl.

2. Shred carrots in a food processor or with a hand grater. Add to the bowl with the cabbage.

3. Place water, tofu, sugar, granulated onion, shallots, vinegar, mustard, salt and black pepper in a food processor and process until smooth.

4. Sprinkle celery seed over cabbage and carrots. Pour on dressing and toss vegetables to coat.

5. Allow coleslaw to marinate for at least 20 minutes

YIELD: 8 SERVINGS

Per serving: 66 Calories, 0.5g Fat, 0.1g Saturated Fat, 0g Cholesterol, 2.6g Protein, 15g Carbohydrate, 3.6g Fiber, 88mg Sodium

FRENCH FRIES

3 tablespoons potato starch

1 tablespoon granulated garlic

1 tablespoon granulated onion

2 teaspoons paprika

½ teaspoon cracked black pepper

½ teaspoon sea salt

6 baking potatoes

canola oil cooking spray

1. Preheat oven to 400°.

2. In a small bowl, combine potato starch, garlic, onion, paprika, black pepper and salt and mix well.

3. Rinse potatoes and scrub to remove all dirt. Do not peel. Cut each potato into ½" slices. Then stack the slices and cut the long way into ½" strips. (*You can also cut them shoestring size, if you prefer.*)

4. Place potatoes in a large bowl and sprinkle with dry ingredients. Shake bowl and toss potatoes to distribute seasonings evenly.

5. Lightly spray a large baking sheet with cooking spray.

6. Distribute potato strips in one layer on prepared sheet and bake in preheated oven about 25 minutes. Flip the fries over and continue to bake until golden brown on the outside, soft on the inside and crunchy, about 20 minutes more.

YIELD: 6 SERVINGS

Per serving: 116 Calories, 0.2g Fat, 0.1g Saturated Fat, 0g Cholesterol, 2.2g Protein, 27g Carbohydrate, 1.7g Fiber, 199mg Sodium

ABOUT FATS

Fat has two functions in the food supply – it provides calories and it enhances taste. Increased caloric intake is important in societies where people work hard and are widely exposed to infectious disease and poor sanitation. In the United States and other developed countries, nutritional-deficiency diseases like rickets, beriberi and scurvy have been eliminated by food fortification, so fat intake in not essential.

Unfortunately, fat consumption in the developed world has increased significantly in this century. The increase comes from the consumption of red meat and high-fat snack foods as well as from hidden fats in vegetable oil, margarine, butter and processed baked goods. The taste-enhancing properties of fat guarantee that higher-fat foods compete more successfully for consumer acceptance than lower-fat foods. High dietary fat intake has become an indicator of a rich, modern Western food supply.

The most important thing you can do to lower your dietary fat and calories is to consider giving up red meat, including veal, beef, pork and lamb. Even when the visible fat is trimmed away, fat lurks between the muscles fibers. A 9- to 14-ounce slab of prime rib can contain more than 1,200 calories and 50 grams of fat. The Department of Agriculture says a normal serving of meat should be a 3-ounce portion.

Some fish are fatty as well. Much of the salmon, trout and catfish sold in stores and restaurants is farm-raised and higher in fat content than fish caught in the wild.

Nuts are also high in fat. A good way to trim the fat from your diet is to minimize the consumption of nuts of all kinds, including peanuts and peanut butter, macadamia nuts and pistachios.

PINTO BEAN QUESADILLAS

These quesadillas make a filling lunch. You can cut them into small triangles and serve as hors d'oeuvres. Use fat-free canned refried beans instead of making your own to save time. (*Low-sodium beans are preferable.*)

- ½ cup dried pinto beans (2 cups cooked)
- ¼ cup chopped cilantro
- 3 vine-ripened tomatoes, diced small
- ¼ teaspoon ground cumin
- ⅛ teaspoon sea salt
- 4 fat-free flour tortillas
- 8 ounces fat-free jack-style soy cheese, grated by hand (about 1 cup)
  canola oil cooking spray
- 1 recipe Pea-camole (see right)
- 1 recipe Roasted Tomato Salsa (page 54) with the following changes: replace the chives with cilantro and squeeze in the juice of 1 lime.

1. Place beans in a saucepan and cover with water. Cook over high heat until beans are tender, about 1½ hours. Drain. (*You can make these a day ahead.*)

2. Place beans in a bowl and mash with a spoon. The mixture should look chunky.

3. Add cilantro and tomatoes to beans. Mix well.

4. Stir in cumin and salt.

5. Place a tortilla on your work surface. Spread ¼ of the bean mixture over half the tortilla. Top with ¼ cup grated soy cheese and fold the tortilla in half. Repeat with remaining tortillas.

6. Spray a griddle or a large sauté pan once with cooking spray. Heat over medium heat and toast filled tortillas on each side as you would a grilled cheese sandwich.

7. Cut quesadillas into 4 equal triangles. Serve with Pea-camole and Roasted Tomato Salsa made with cilantro and lime.

YIELD: 4 QUESADILLAS

Per serving: 403 Calories, 4.3g Fat, 0.7g Saturated Fat, 0g Cholesterol, 27.9g Protein, 64g Carbohydrate, 12.5g Fiber, 916mg Sodium

PEA-CAMOLE

- 4 cups frozen peas
- 2 tablespoons water
  juice of 2 limes
- 1 tablespoon low-fat silken tofu
- ½ teaspoon sea salt
- ¼ teaspoon ground cumin
- ¼ teaspoon chili powder
- ¼ cup diced tomato
- ¼ cup diced onion
- 2 tablespoons chopped cilantro

1. Cook frozen peas in boiling water until soft, about 10 minutes

2. Place peas, water, lime juice, tofu, salt, cumin and chili powder in a food processor and process until smooth.

3. Scrape mixture into a bowl. Add tomatoes, onions and cilantro and mix.

4. Serve as a garnish for any Southwestern or Mexican entree, or serve by itself with salsa and chips.

YIELD: 3 CUPS

Per 2-tablespoon serving: 18 Calories, 0.1g Fat, 0g Saturated Fat, 0g Cholesterol, 1.2g Protein, 3g Carbohydrate, 1.2g Fiber, 68mg Sodium

TOFU EGG SALAD SANDWICH

This recipe looks exactly like the more conventional kind of egg salad. You can make your own fat-free tofu mayonnaise or purchase one at a health food market.

MAYONNAISE

- ½ cup low-fat silken tofu (4 ounces)
- 2 tablespoons water
- 2 tablespoons fresh lemon juice
- 1 tablespoon Dijon mustard
- 1 teaspoon natural cane sugar or fructose
- 1 tablespoon powdered egg white
- ⅛ teaspoon sea salt
  ground black pepper to taste

SANDWICHES

- 1 recipe tofu mayonnaise (above)
- 1 teaspoon Dijon mustard
- 1 teaspoon granulated onion
- ½ teaspoon turmeric
- ½ teaspoon dried oregano
- ¼ teaspoon dried tarragon or ½ teaspoon fresh
- ⅛ teaspoon granulated garlic
- ⅛ teaspoon sea salt
  black pepper to taste
- 1 pound or 1 block firm low-fat tofu (2 cups)
- ½ cup celery diced or coarsely chopped
- 1 tablespoon diced or coarsely chopped green onions
- 1 shallot, chopped
- 8 slices fat-free whole wheat bread
- 2 large carrots, grated (about 1¼ cups)
- 1 cup clover or alfalfa sprouts (or other sprouts of your choice)

TO MAKE MAYONNAISE

1. Place all ingredients in a food processor fitted with a metal blade or in a blender and process until smooth.

2. Store in a container and refrigerate up to 3 days, until ready to use.

TO MAKE SANDWICHES

1. Combine Tofu Mayonnaise, mustard, granulated onion, turmeric, oregano, tarragon, granulated garlic, salt and pepper in a mixing bowl.

2. Place tofu in a smaller bowl and crumble with your hands until it is the texture of mashed eggs. Add it to the mayonnaise mixture and stir.

3. Stir in celery, green onions and shallots.

4. Place 4 slices of bread on your work surface. (*Toast the bread first, if you prefer.*) Layer ¼ of the tofu egg salad, ¼ of the carrots and ¼ of the sprouts on each slice of bread or toast and top with a second slice of bread or toast. Cut sandwiches in half and serve.

YIELD: 4 SANDWICHES

Per serving: 230 Calories, 4.6g Fat, 0.8g Saturated Fat, 0g Cholesterol, 16.5g Protein, 35g Carbohydrate, 6.9g Fiber, 622mg Sodium

SPICES

Two staples from the world of spicy foods—curcumin, which is found in cumin and turmeric and the curry powders that use them, and capsaicin, found in some of the hottest chili peppers—help inhibit the development of certain cancers.

Curcumin provides the yellow pigment in turmeric, which has been used as both a coloring agent and a spice since as early as 600 B.C. Turmeric caught the eye of Marco Polo, who in 1280 described it as "Indian saffron." It was subsequently brought back to Europe and used as an inexpensive substitute for saffron in many recipes. Turmeric is also widely used in the cuisines of India and Mexico.

Curcumin is also found in the cumin seed, a spice cultivated in the Nile Valley as far back as 1550 B.C. Cumin is widely used in Mediterranean, Indian, Middle Eastern and Mexican cooking—and is a key spice in many varieties of American chili.

Researchers believe curcumin fights bacteria, fungi and cholesterol—and without side effects. Curcumin has been found to relieve sufferers of skin cancer by reducing the smell, discharge and itching often associated with the disease, and to fight colon cancer by increasing the natural adrenal production of cortisone. It also relieves pain and inflammation from workouts and premenstrual cramps.

As much as we now associate searingly hot chili peppers with the cuisines of Asia, it was not until the 16th century that these peppers made their way east. Indigenous to Central and South America and the West Indies, the fiery chilies appealed to Portuguese explorers who carried them to India, Macao and Africa. This introduction of foreign ingredients transformed the food of parts of China (most notably Szechwan and Hunan provinces), Korea, Vietnam, Thailand, Malaysia and Indonesia.

In addition to its cancer-fighting properties, capsaicin is a natural decongestant (your nose runs when you consume lots of it) and is used in some skin ointments. Applied sparingly, it can help to relieve internal and external inflammation.

Recent studies have allayed concerns about chili peppers' link to stomach cancer or ulcers. These studies have found that the mild irritation from chilies actually prompts the body to replace cells of the stomach lining.

Serrano

Ancho

Cayenne

Habanero

Pasilla

NEW DELI

This is a hot dog with attitude. Serve with Baked Beans and Broccoli in Soy Cheese Sauce. For smaller appetites, make these sandwiches with only 1 layer of ingredients. For a crunchier sandwich, toast the bread first instead of grilling the finished sandwich.

- 4 Roma or other plum tomatoes
- 1 large onion, roasted (page 76) or raw, peeled and sliced lengthwise
- 8 fat-free tofu hot dogs
- 8 slices fat-free rye or sourdough bread
- 1/4 cup yellow mustard
- 1 cup sauerkraut, drained
-   canola oil cooking spray

1. Cut tomatoes lengthwise into 4 equal slices. Set aside.

2. If not using a roasted onion, spray a sauté pan with cooking spray. Cook onion over low heat until tender and light brown in color, about 10 minutes. Set aside.

3. Slit tofu hot dogs lengthwise. Spray a griddle or large sauté pan once with cooking spray. Spread hot dogs open and grill, slit-side down, for 2 minutes. Set aside.

4. Spread the bread slices with mustard and lay out 4 of them on your work surface. (Set aside the remaining 4.) Place 1 tofu dog, split open, on each slice. Add 2 slices of tomato, 1/4 cup sauerkraut, 1/4 of the sliced onions, another 2 slices of tomato, another tofu dog and close with a slice of bread.

5. Spray the griddle or sauté pan once with cooking spray and grill sandwiches on both sides until toasted. Slice in half and serve.

YIELD: 4 SANDWICHES

Per serving: 284 Calories, 2.8g Fat, 0.4g Saturated Fat, 0g Cholesterol, 28.6g Protein, 38g Carbohydrate, 6.4g Fiber, 1575mg Sodium

BAKED BEANS

- 2 1/2 cups dried white beans (navy or pea beans)
- 2 cups nonfat barbecue sauce
- 1 cup ketchup
- 1/2 cup water
- 2 tablespoons maple syrup
- 2 shallots, peeled (about 2 tablespoons chopped)
- 1 tablespoon prepared yellow mustard
- 1 tablespoon molasses
- 2 pieces vegetarian Canadian bacon or smoky tempeh strips, diced

1. Soak beans overnight in 6 cups of water. The next day, drain the water and place beans in large saucepan with water to cover. Bring water to a boil, turn down to a simmer.

2. Cook until beans are just tender, about 1 1/2 hours. Drain. Beans can be prepared up to this point 24 hours ahead.

3. Preheat oven to 350°.

4. Place remaining ingredients except bacon in a food processor fitted with a metal blade and process until smooth. Scrape mixture into bowl with beans and stir until beans are thoroughly coated. Stir in diced bacon.

5. Transfer beans to a heavy casserole dish. Cover with foil. Bake in preheated oven until beans are soft, about 2 1/2 to 3 hours, stirring every 30 minutes. If mixture becomes too dry during the baking, stir in a little water. Serve or refrigerate up to 5 days.

YIELD: 6 CUPS

Per half-cup serving: 201 Calories, 1.4g Fat, 0.2g Saturated Fat, 0g Cholesterol, 10.7g Protein, 38g Carbohydrate, 7.8g Fiber, 613mg Sodium

VLT WITH HERB MUSTARD

This is a remake of the classic BLT. Serve with
Mashed Potatoes (page 81) and Creamed Spinach (see right).

- ½ cup yellow mustard
- 1 tablespoon snipped fresh or dried chives
- 1 tablespoon chopped fresh parsley
- ⅛ teaspoon cracked black pepper
- 8 leaves romaine, washed and dried
- 8 slices fat-free bread of your choice
- 4 Roma or other plum tomatoes, sliced lengthwise into 4 equal slices
- 1 pound fat-free tofu bologna slices

1. Place mustard in a small bowl.

2. Add chives, parsley and black pepper to mustard and mix well. Set aside until ready to use.

3. Tear romaine leaves to fit bread slices. Set aside.

4. Place 4 slices of bread on your work surface. Spread bread with herb mustard. Add to each slice ¼ of the bologna slices, 4 slices of tomato and 2 romaine leaves. Top with another slice of bread. Cut sandwiches in half and serve.

YIELD: **4 SANDWICHES**

Per serving: 305 Calories, 3.4g Fat, 0.5g Saturated Fat, 0.5g Cholesterol, 32.9g Protein, 35g Carbohydrate, 3.3g Fiber, 1460mg Sodium

ROASTED ONION

Using roasted onions in place of fried ones will add flavor
to your dishes without adding fat. Place onions, unpeeled,
on a baking dish and bake at 350 degrees until soft, about
45 minutes. They will keep in the refrigerator for about 1
week. When you're ready to use the onion, peel and prepare
according to the recipe. Shallots may be prepared the same
way; roast for 25 minutes.

CREAMED SPINACH

- 2 tablespoons cornstarch
- 1 cup plain 1% soy milk
- 4 cups spinach, well rinsed and trimmed (or two 10-ounce bags washed spinach)
- 1 sliced onion, roasted (see left) or raw
- ¼ cup low-fat silken tofu (2 ounces)
- 2 teaspoons granulated onion
- ½ teaspoon brewer's yeast flakes
- ¼ teaspoon grated nutmeg
- ⅛ teaspoon sea salt
  dash white pepper, optional
  canola oil cooking spray (if using raw onion)

1. Put a large pot of water over high heat and bring to a boil.

2. Meanwhile, place cornstarch in a small saucepan. Slowly pour in soy milk stirring constantly, to blend. Set over medium heat and bring to a boil. Continue stirring constantly and cook until sauce is thick, about 10 minutes. Remove from heat and set aside.

3. Blanch spinach for 1 minute in prepared pot of boiling water. Drain immediately and press out excess liquid.

4. If not using a roasted onion, spray a sauté pan with cooking spray and cook thinly sliced raw onion over low heat until light brown, about 10 minutes. Set aside.

5. Place spinach, onion, tofu, granulated onion, brewer's yeast and nutmeg in a food processor. Process thoroughly.

6. In a saucepan combine spinach mixture and cream sauce. Cook over low heat, stirring occasionally, until hot.

7. Season with salt and add white pepper if desired. Serve.

YIELD: **6 SERVINGS**

Per serving: 62 Calories, 0.8g Fat, 0.2g Saturated Fat, 0g Cholesterol, 3.5g Protein, 12g Carbohydrate, 2.5g Fiber, 131mg Sodium

CRUCIFEROUS
VEGETABLES

In regions where consumption of cruciferous vegetables—broccoli, Brussels sprouts, cabbage, kale, cauliflower, bok choy—is high, rates of some cancers are lower. The vegetables have been widely available for thousands of years. Broccoli was a favorite food in Rome 2,000 years ago, and historians believe that Italian immigrants introduced broccoli to the United States 200 years ago.

More recently, scientists have determined that broccoli and other cruciferous vegetables contain sulforaphane, which increases the activities of enzymes that deactivate cancer-causing chemicals. One study has found that three-day-old sprouts from broccoli seeds possess 30 to 50 times the amount of sulforaphane of regular broccoli.

Most research has focused on how these substances combat breast cancer and colon cancer. No specific evidence has emerged of an impact on prostate cancer, but research continues.

Brussels sprouts are rich in compounds such as cyanohydroxybutene that might be effective in preventing cancer. Chinese cabbage, a slightly longer and more compacted head of light green cabbage, contains the compound brassinin, which may also fight cancer by affecting the action of hormones in the body. An experiment with laboratory rats showed a decreased incidence of cancer after consumption of a compound found in cauliflower and broccoli.

BROCCOLI IN SOY CHEESE SAUCE

1 head broccoli (about 1 pound)

SOY CHEESE SAUCE

1 teaspoon cornstarch

2 tablespoons water

1 cup plain 1% soy milk

6 ounces nonfat mozzarella- style or jack-style soy cheese, grated by hand (about 3/4 cup)

1 teaspoon granulated onion

3/4 teaspoon turmeric

1/8 teaspoon grated nutmeg

dash cayenne, if desired

TO MAKE BROCCOLI

1. Preheat oven to 350°. Place a large saucepan of water over high heat and bring to a boil.

2. Cut most of stems from broccoli, leaving about 2" of stem attached to florets. Cut into 6 equal portions. (*Bag and freeze unused stem portions for soup.*)

3. Add broccoli to the boiling water and cook for 2 minutes, uncovered.

4. Drain water all at once and run cold water over the broccoli to stop the cooking process. Add several ice cubes to the cooling water.

TO MAKE SOY CHEESE SAUCE

1. Dissolve the cornstarch in water.

2. Place soy milk, cheese, granulated onion, turmeric and nutmeg in a saucepan and bring to a boil stirring frequently. Turn heat down to a simmer, continuing to stir frequently until cheese is melted.

3. Stir cornstarch mixture. Add to sauce, increase heat to medium and stir constantly until sauce thickens.

4. Remove pan from heat and season sauce with cayenne, if desired.

TO ASSEMBLE DISH

1. Place broccoli in a baking dish and cover with cheese sauce.

2. Cover baking dish with foil.

3. Bake in preheated oven until broccoli is hot and sauce is bubbling, about 15 to 20 minutes.

YIELD: 6 SERVINGS

Per serving: 123 Calories, 0.6g Fat, 0.1g Saturated Fat, 0g Cholesterol, 10.9g Protein, 12g Carbohydrate, 3.3g Fiber, 276mg Sodium

CAULIFLOWER AU GRATIN

- 1 head cauliflower, cut into 6 portions
- 1 recipe Soy Cheese Sauce (facing page)
- ½ cup dried fat-free herb bread crumbs

1. Preheat oven to 350°.

2. Bring a large saucepan of water to a boil. Cook cauliflower for 3 minutes. Drain. Place cauliflower in a small rectangular baking dish.

3. Pour Soy Cheese Sauce over cauliflower and sprinkle with bread crumbs.

4. Cover with foil and bake in preheated oven until cheese sauce is bubbling, about 25 minutes.

YIELD: 6 SERVINGS

Per serving: 151 Calories, 1g Fat, 0.1g Saturated Fat, 0g Cholesterol, 10.4g Protein, 17g Carbohydrate, 2.5g Fiber, 427mg Sodium

GRILLED BRUSSELS SPROUTS

If you have a vegetable-grilling tray with small openings, use it for this recipe. Try the grilling sauce on tofu, fish, chicken or any vegetable.

- 2 cups Brussels sprouts (washed, trimmed and cut in half lengthwise)

FOR GRILLING SAUCE

- ½ cup ketchup
- ¼ cup low-sodium tamari soy sauce
- 1 tablespoon honey
- ½" piece fresh ginger, peeled and grated or minced
- 2 teaspoons crushed fresh garlic (about 4 cloves)

1. In a pot of boiling water blanch Brussels sprouts for 3 minutes. Strain water in a colander and rinse Brussels sprouts with cold water.

2. Place all ingredients for grilling sauce in a food processor and process until smooth.

3. Coat Brussels sprouts with sauce. (You can put sprouts in a mixing bowl, pour sauce overall and mix with a spoon or spatula.) Preheat barbecue.

4. Arrange Brussels sprouts flat-side down over medium flame on barbecue grill. Grill 2 minutes. Turn sprouts and grill 2 minutes longer. Serve.

YIELD: 6 SERVINGS

Per serving: 61 Calories, 0.3g Fat, 0.1g Saturated Fat, 0g Cholesterol, 2.9g Protein, 14.1g Carbohydrate, 2.9g Fiber, 649mg Sodium

YAM BRÛLÉE

4 medium yams, peeled
and cut into 8 pieces each

1 vanilla bean, optional

2 teaspoons maple syrup

¼ teaspoon vanilla extract

2 tablespoons maple or natural cane sugar

1. Preheat broiler.

2. Place yams in a large pot, cover with water and bring to a boil over medium high heat.

3. Cook yams in boiling water until soft, about 25 minutes. Drain

4. Transfer yams to a food processor or the bowl of an electric mixer and purée for about 2 minutes, until mixture is smooth.

5. If using vanilla bean, split it down the middle, open the pod and scrape the beans into the purée using a sharp knife. (*Reserve vanilla bean pod to flavor another recipe; wrap it airtight and freeze.*)

6. Add maple syrup and vanilla extract to mixture and purée for 30 seconds more.

7. Divide yam mixture among 6 individual custard dishes. Coat the surface of each with maple or natural sugar.

8. Place custard dishes on a baking sheet and set under broiler until sugar melts and bubbles, about 5 minutes. Watch carefully and remove before sugar begins to burn.

YIELD: 6 SERVINGS

Per serving: 100 Calories, 0.1g Fat, 0g Saturated Fat, 0g Cholesterol, 1.3g Protein, 24g Carbohydrate, 2.3g Fiber, 9mg Sodium

STEWED TOMATOES

3 pounds fresh Roma or other vine-ripened tomatoes

2 tablespoons water

1 teaspoon granulated onion

1 teaspoon granulated garlic

1 teaspoon dried basil

1 teaspoon dried oregano

½ teaspoon dried thyme

⅛ teaspoon sea salt
ground black pepper to taste

1. Core tomatoes and quarter them.

2. Place all ingredients in a saucepan and cook over low heat, stirring occasionally, until tomatoes are soft, about 20 minutes.

YIELD: 6 CUPS

Per serving: 51 Calories, 0.8g Fat, 0.1g Saturated Fat, 0g Cholesterol, 2g Protein, 11g Carbohydrate, 1.9g Fiber, 68mg Sodium

CORN AND BUTTERNUT SQUASH

1 medium butternut squash

4 ears corn on the cob

1 15-ounce can corn

1 teaspoon Spike seasoning or ⅛ teaspoon each sea salt and freshly ground black pepper)

1. Preheat oven to 350°. Fill a large pot with water and bring to a boil.

2. Place butternut squash on a baking sheet. Pierce several times with a sharp knife. Bake in preheated oven until tender, about 1½ hours. Allow to cool at least 30 minutes. (*This can be done a day ahead.*)

3. Place corn in boiling water and blanch 2 minutes. Remove from water.

4. Use a serrated knife to cut kernels off cob.

5. Skin and seed butternut squash.

6. Place squash and drained canned corn in food processor and purée.

7. Transfer squash mixture to a mixing bowl, fold in corn kernels and stir in Spike seasoning.

8. Spoon mixture into a casserole dish and cover with foil.

9. Bake in preheated oven until heated through, about 30 minutes.

YIELD: 6 SERVINGS

Per serving: 186 Calories, 1.9g Fat, 0.3g Saturated Fat, 0g Cholesterol, 5.5g Protein, 44g Carbohydrate, 5.1g Fiber, 295mg Sodium

APPLESAUCE

- 1 vanilla bean, optional
- 8 large apples, peeled, cored and quartered
- 3/4 cup water
- 1 tablespoon maple or natural cane sugar, optional
- 1 teaspoon cinnamon
- 1 teaspoon vanilla extract

1. If using vanilla bean, split it lengthwise and use a sharp knife to scrape seeds into a large saucepan. Add bean pod to pan as well.

2. Add remaining ingredients to pan and place over medium high heat.

3. Bring to a boil and turn down to a simmer.

4. Cover pan and simmer until apples are soft, about 20 minutes.

5. Remove bean pod and transfer apple mixture to food processor work bowl.

6. Purée, using on/off pulses, until sauce reaches desired consistency. (*This can be chunky or smooth.*)

YIELD: 6 CUPS

Per 1-cup serving: 153 Calories, 0.8g Fat, 0.1g Saturated Fat, 0g Cholesterol, 0.4g Protein, 39g Carbohydrate, 5.2g Fiber, 0mg Sodium

MASHED POTATOES

- 4 large baking potatoes
- 3/4 cup plain 1% soy milk
- 1 teaspoon granulated onion
- 3/4-1 teaspoon sea salt
- 1/2 teaspoon granulated garlic
- 1/8 teaspoon ground black pepper

1. Peel and cut potatoes into 6 or 8 pieces.

2. Place potatoes in a pot with water to cover. Place pot over medium-high heat and bring to a rolling boil.

3. Continue boiling potatoes until they are soft, but not mushy, about 20 to 25 minutes.

4. Drain potatoes and transfer to the bowl of an electric mixer or use a hand mixer. (*The hotter the potatoes, the less likely you are to end up with lumps.*)

5. Beat potatoes on high speed for 1 minute. Turn down to low speed and slowly add soy milk. Turn off mixer and scrape down sides of bowl.

6. Add seasonings and beat again on high speed for 1 minute. Serve.

YIELD: 6 SERVINGS

Per serving: 122 Calories, 0.4g Fat, 0.1g Saturated Fat, 0g Cholesterol, 2.5g Protein, 28g Carbohydrate, 2.2g Fiber, 312mg Sodium

break

f a s t s

AND

SHAKES

supply

HUNGRY

bodies

with

ALL-DAY **energy.**

Don't leave home without them.

FRUIT SHAKE

Shakes are a great way to incorporate soy into your diet. Plan to have at least 1 a day.

- ½ cup orange, apple or mixed fruit juice
- ½ cup brewed organic green tea or fruit juice
- ¼ cup berries of your choice
- 1 banana
- 1 teaspoon grated lemon zest
- 1 teaspoon grated orange zest
- ½ cup strawberry or plain soy protein isolate powder
- 3 capsules green tea power, optional
  (*open capsules and use powder only*)

1. Place all ingredients in blender container and blend thoroughly.

YIELD: 1 SHAKE

Per serving: 265 Calories, 1.7g Fat, 0.2g Saturated Fat, 0g Cholesterol, 22.1g Protein, 42g Carbohydrate, 3.3g Fiber, 207mg Sodium

CHOCOLATE SHAKE

- ½ cup orange juice
- ½ cup brewed organic green tea
- 2 strawberries, hulled
- 1 banana
- ½ cup chocolate soy protein isolate powder
- 1 teaspoon grated orange zest
- 1 teaspoon grated lemon zest
- 3 capsules green tea power
  (*open capsules and use powder only*)

1. Place all ingredients in blender container and blend thoroughly.

YIELD: 1 SHAKE

Per serving: 283 Calories, 1.6g Fat, 0.2g Saturated Fat, 0g Cholesterol, 22g Protein, 42g Carbohydrate, 3.2g Fiber, 207mg Sodium

EGGS MICHAEL

This is a fat-free remake of Eggs Benedict. It makes an elegant presentation served with sliced tomatoes and steamed asparagus. For Eggs Florentine, replace the vegetarian Canadian bacon with steamed spinach. You will need an egg poacher for this recipe; egg whites will separate if you poach them in hot water. If you do not have an egg poacher, simply scramble the egg whites and then proceed with the recipe. To make a Fruit Sandwich garnish, layer three fruit slices and trim the edges to form a triangular stack.

- **16 egg whites or 2 cups nonfat egg substitute**
- **4 English muffin halves**
- **4 pieces fat-free vegetarian Canadian bacon**
- **¼ recipe Soy Cheese Sauce (page 78), kept warm, with a piece of plastic wrap directly on top, to prevent a skin from forming**
- **canola oil cooking spray**

1. Preheat oven to 350°. Bring a pot of water to a simmer. If your poacher is not nonstick, spray once with cooking spray.

2. Place egg whites in poacher and cook over simmering water until solid, about 5 minutes

3. While eggs are poaching, toast English muffins and warm bacon in the oven for 2 minutes.

4. Place a muffin half on a plate and top with bacon. Place a poached egg on top of the muffin and coat with warm Soy Cheese Sauce. Serve

YIELD: 4 SERVINGS

Per serving: 222 Calories, 1.7g Fat, 0.4g Saturated Fat, 0g Cholesterol, 22.7g Protein, 21g Carbohydrate, 1.2g Fiber, 587mg Sodium

BLUEBERRY BANANA MULTI-GRAIN PANCAKES

You can use this batter as the base for any fruit pancake. To make Cinnamon Apple Pancakes, add 1 teaspoon cinnamon and the cooked apples from the Apple Pie recipe (page 99). Or experiment with other types of fruit. The teaspoon of applesauce is a fat-replacement. If you don't have applesauce, you may substitute a teaspoon of crushed canned pears or other puréed fruit. As a flavorful accompaniment, add grated orange zest and 1 or 2 leftover vanilla bean pods (scraped out and saved from another recipe) to a bottle of maple syrup. Store in the refrigerator overnight or longer before serving with the pancakes of your choice. Offer soysage alongside the pancakes to recreate an old-fashioned Sunday breakfast.

- ⅓ cup whole wheat pastry flour
- ⅓ cup oat flour
- ⅓ cup unbleached flour
- 2 teaspoons baking powder
- ¼ teaspoon sea salt
- 1 cup 1% vanilla soy milk
- ¼ cup egg whites (2 or 3 large whites) or ¼ cup nonfat egg substitute
- 1 teaspoon vanilla extract
- 1 teaspoon grated orange zest
- 1 teaspoon unsweetened applesauce
  canola oil cooking spray
- 2 bananas
- 1 cup fresh or frozen blueberries

1. In a mixing bowl, combine flours, baking powder and salt.

2. In another bowl, mix together soy milk, egg whites, vanilla, orange zest and applesauce.

3. Combine wet ingredients with dry ingredients and mix well.

4. Slice bananas and wash blueberries, if fresh.

5. Set a nonstick griddle or a sauté pan over medium-low heat. Allow to warm for 2 minutes. When it is heated, spray once with cooking spray. Use a spoon or small ladle to drop onto griddle mounds of batter that spread into circles about 3" across.

6. When small bubbles appear on the surface of the pancakes, add 3 slices of banana and 5 or 6 blueberries to each pancake. Allow to settle for about 30 seconds, then flip pancake.

7. Cook for about 2 minutes and serve with warm maple or fruit syrup. (*Maple syrup has a lot of calories so use sparingly.*)

YIELD: 4 SERVINGS (12 PANCAKES)

Per serving: 209 Calories, 1.8g Fat, 0.3g Saturated Fat, 0g Cholesterol, 6.5g Protein, 43g Carbohydrate, 4.4g Fiber, 557mg Sodium

CINNAMON WHOLE-GRAIN WAFFLES WITH STRAWBERRIES AND RASPBERRIES

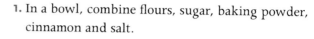

This waffle recipe can be adapted according to your taste and the ingredients you have on hand. Substitute other grain flours, if you like, or serve with any fruit that appeals to you. For a change, serve with apple or pear butter rather than syrup.

- 2/3 **cup whole wheat pastry flour**
- 2/3 **cup oat flour**
- 2/3 **cup unbleached flour**
- 2 **tablespoons maple sugar or natural cane sugar**
- 2 **teaspoons baking powder**
- 1 **teaspoon cinnamon**
- 1/2 **teaspoon sea salt**
- 2 **cups 1% vanilla soy milk**
- 1/4 **cup nonfat egg substitute**
- 5 **teaspoons applesauce**
- 1 **teaspoon vanilla extract**
- 1 **teaspoon grated orange zest**
- 2 **egg whites**
- 1 **cup fresh strawberries, washed and hulled**
- 1 **cup fresh raspberries**
  canola oil cooking spray

1. In a bowl, combine flours, sugar, baking powder, cinnamon and salt.

2. In another bowl, combine soy milk, egg substitute, applesauce, vanilla extract and orange zest.

3. Add wet ingredients to dry ingredients. Mix well.

4. Beat egg whites with an electric mixer until soft peaks form. Fold gently into batter.

5. Spray a waffle iron lightly with cooking spray. Pour 1/4 cup batter onto preheated waffle iron. Cook about 3 minutes, until waffle is brown and firm..

6. Remove from waffle iron and serve, topped with strawberries, raspberries and a little maple syrup.

YIELD: 4 SERVINGS

Per serving: 311 Calories, 1.9g Fat, 0.7g Saturated Fat, 0g Cholesterol, 11.4g Protein, 39g Carbohydrate, 6.8g Fiber, 646mg Sodium

CORN TOMATO OMELET WITH FRESH PARSLEY

This is a classic omelet prepared without egg yolks. For a change, substitute the vegetables of your choice. To spice it up, add 1 or 2 minced jalapeño peppers along with the other vegetables. Serve with fresh fruit and fat-free toast and jelly.

- **24 egg whites or 3 cups nonfat egg substitute**
- **⅛ teaspoon sea salt**
- **black pepper to taste**
- **2 ears fresh corn**
- **½ bunch chopped fresh parsley**
- **2 vine-ripened tomatoes, diced small**
- **8 ounces fat-free mozzarella-style soy cheese, grated by hand (about 1 cup)**
- **canola oil cooking spray**

1. Place egg whites in a bowl and season with salt and pepper. Beat slightly.

2. Bring a pot of water to a boil and blanch corn for 2 minutes.

3. Strip kernels from cobs with a serrated knife and set aside. Preheat broiler.

4. Lightly spray an ovenproof nonstick omelet pan with cooking spray and place over medium heat. Pour ⅙ of the egg mixture (about ½ cup) into the pan and scramble with a rubber spatula until egg is almost solid, about 90 seconds.

5. Press on the egg with a spatula to flatten out like a tortilla. Place ⅙ of the corn kernels, ⅙ of the cheese, ⅙ of the tomatoes and ⅙ of the parsley over half of the omelet.

6. Place under broiler until cheese is melted, about 30 seconds. Fold over and roll onto a plate. Repeat 5 times. Serve with fresh fruit and toast.

YIELD: **6 SERVINGS**

Per serving: 166 Calories, 0.7g Fat, 0.1g Saturated Fat, 0g Cholesterol, 23.4g Protein, 16g Carbohydrate, 1.7g Fiber, 572mg Sodium

CHERRY VANILLA GRANOLA

Serve this fat-free, crunchy cereal with chilled soy milk or fat-free yogurt. For a spectacular presentation, serve in a wine glass layered with yogurt and fruit—a granola parfait.

- **3 cups oatmeal**
- **¼ cup oat bran**
- **1 cup maple syrup**
- **1 teaspoon vanilla extract**
- **½ teaspoon cinnamon**
- **½ cup dried cherries**
- **¼ cup raisins**
- **2 tablespoons maple sugar**
- **canola oil cooking spray**

1. Preheat oven to 350°. Spray a baking sheet or jelly roll pan once with cooking spray.

2. Mix oatmeal, oat bran, maple syrup, vanilla extract and cinnamon together in a large bowl. Spread on prepared baking sheet and bake in preheated oven 15 minutes. Toss mixture with a spatula so the edges do not burn.

3. Continue to bake until golden brown, about 15 minutes longer. Transfer to a bowl to cool.

4. Add cherries, raisins and maple sugar and toss.

5. Store in an airtight container for up to 1 month.

YIELD: **4 CUPS**

Per half-cup: 288 Calories, 2.5g Fat, 0.4g Saturated Fat, 0g Cholesterol, 6.3g Protein, 64g Carbohydrate, 4.2g Fiber, 9mg Sodium

PORTION CONTROL

A HEALTHY diet means not just eating the right foods but the right amounts, too. And while there's considerable flexibility in a well-designed diet, portion control needs to be at the core.

Unfortunately, several currents in American eating habits can carry you in the wrong direction. All-you-can-eat buffets. Restaurants that offer 40-ounce steaks and four-pound lobsters. Giant bowls of pasta. Convenience stores that offer a 64-ounce "cup" of soda—really more like a bucket. Vast tubs of popcorn at the movies. Sandwiches so bulging that the top slice of bread needs to be pinned on.

Even some "health food" is oversized, like those swollen low-fat muffins bursting from their tins. The small print on the label might warn you that one muffin equals two servings. Even when locally baked muffins (and brownies and cookies, too) are labeled, studies have found that they are consistently 20 percent larger than their labels say.

Is it any wonder that people eat too much? As recently as 1980, one in four Americans was overweight. Now it's one in three. Guidelines from the Department of Agriculture and the Food and Drug Administration suggest that the typical restaurant portion is two to three times too large. A typical tuna sandwich, for instance, contains 11 ounces of tuna salad; the recommended portion is 4 ounces.

Even plates are getting bigger. In department stores and restaurants, the standard dinner plate has grown in the last decade to 11¼ inches across, from 10¼ inches—and many restaurants prefer a 12-inch plate.

RECOMMENDED PORTIONS:

VEGETABLES
1 cup of raw leafy vegetables
½ cup of other vegetables—cooked or chopped raw
¾ cup of vegetable juice

FRUIT
1 medium apple, banana, orange
½ cup of chopped, cooked or canned fruit
¾ cup of fruit juice

BREAD, CEREAL, RICE AND PASTA
1 slice of bread
1 ounce of ready-to-eat cereal
½ cup of cooked cereal, rice and pasta

MEAT, POULTRY, FISH, DRY BEANS, EGGS AND NUTS
2-3 ounces of cooked lean meat, poultry or fish
½ cup of cooked dry beans
1 egg
2 tablespoons of peanut butter

The problem simply is that if you eat more than your body needs, the extra calories are stored as fat. This starts you in the direction of being overweight and can lead to obesity. A wealth of scientific evidence demonstrates that obesity contributes to many diseases, including prostate cancer.

The remedy is obvious: self-control. If a sandwich is far too large, eat only half and have the rest wrapped for another meal. Faced with an immense order of pasta, immediately resolve to ask for a doggie bag to bring some home. Or plan a meal around sharing entrees. Don't eat bread steadily until your food is served. Drink a glass of water as soon as you're seated.

Restaurants are nudging you in the other direction, offering larger portions for a few cents more (or a second pizza at a steep discount). That may seem like good value, but it's never a bargain for your body to consume more food than you need.

dess

turn the
SIMPLEST
MEALS

into SWEET

(and healthy)

CELEBRATIONS.

Healthy recipes leave you smiling

to the last crumb.

erts

LEMON MERINGUE PIE

This pie looks as good as the mile-high diner version. Try substituting lime juice for the lemon juice and you'll think you're eating Key Lime Pie. No kidding!

GRAHAM CRACKER CRUST

- ½ cup fat-free graham crackers (10 individual crackers)
- 2 cups white or oat flour
- ½ cup maple or natural cane sugar
- ½ cup unsweetened applesauce
- ⅛ cup egg white (about half of 1 white) or nonfat egg substitute
- 1 teaspoon vanilla extract
- ½ teaspoon baking soda
  canola oil cooking spray

LEMON FILLING

- 1½ cups 1% vanilla soy milk
- 1 cup fructose, Fruitsource or natural cane sugar
- ⅓ cup fresh lemon juice
- ¼ cup cornstarch
- 1 tablespoon lemon extract
- 1 teaspoon vanilla extract
- 1 teaspoon grated lemon zest
- 1 vanilla bean, optional
- ¼ cup nonfat egg substitute

MERINGUE

- 5 egg whites
- 6 tablespoons natural cane sugar or Fruitsource
  dash sea salt

TO MAKE THE CRUST

1. Grind graham crackers in a food processor fitted with a metal blade. Add all remaining ingredients and process until mixture forms a ball. Do not overprocess.

2. Remove dough and flatten into a disk. Wrap in plastic wrap and chill thoroughly before rolling, 45 minutes to 1 hour.

3. Preheat oven to 350°. Spray a 9" pie pan once with cooking spray.

4. Flour work surface and roll pie dough into an 11" circle with a floured rolling pin. Place in prepared pie dish and use the tip of a fork to flatten the edges onto the rim of the dish.

5. Bake in preheated oven until light brown, about 15 minutes. While crust is baking, prepare the lemon filling.

TO MAKE THE FILLING

1. Place all filling ingredients except vanilla bean and egg substitute in a saucepan.

2. If using vanilla bean, split it down the center lengthwise. Scrape seeds into the saucepan and add the scraped pod.

3. Cook mixture over medium heat, stirring constantly, until it thickens, about 8 minutes. Remove from heat. Stir a small amount of the hot mixture into the egg substitute, then return this tempered egg substitute mixture to pan. Place back over low heat and cook, stirring constantly, for 5 minutes. Remove vanilla bean pod. Pour mixture into baked pie shell.

4. Refrigerate while making the meringue.

TO MAKE THE MERINGUE

1. Preheat broiler. Place a large pot of water on the stove and bring to a boil.

2. Pour egg whites, sugar and salt into a bowl that will sit securely on top of the pot. Place the bowl over the hot water.

3. Stir constantly until egg whites become warm to the touch.

4. Remove bowl and beat whites with an electric mixer until they reach stiff peaks, about 12 minutes.

5. Spoon mounds of meringue over lemon filling, forming peaks.

6. Place pie under broiler at least 6" from the heat until meringue turns light gold, about 30 seconds. Watch carefully!

YIELD: ONE 9" PIE (10 SERVINGS)

Per serving: 302 Calories, 0.8g Fat, 0.2g Saturated Fat, 0g Cholesterol, 5.7g Protein, 66g Carbohydrate, 1g Fiber, 180mg Sodium

CITRUS RICE PUDDING

over 60 minutes

For an elegant presentation of this favorite comfort food, bake in individual custard dishes.

 3 cups cooked long-grain white rice or 2½ cups cooked long-grain brown rice

 2½ cups 1% vanilla soy milk

 ¾ cup nonfat egg substitute

 ½ cup orange juice (if tangerine juice is available use ¼ cup orange juice and ¼ cup tangerine juice)

 ½ cup fructose, natural cane sugar or liquid fruit sweetener

 ¼ cup raisins

 ¼ cup dried cherries

 1 teaspoon vanilla extract

 1 teaspoon orange extract

 1 teaspoon grated orange zest

 1 teaspoon grated tangerine zest

 1 teaspoon grated lemon zest

 1 teaspoon grated lime zest

 1 vanilla bean, optional

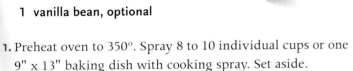

1. Preheat oven to 350°. Spray 8 to 10 individual cups or one 9" x 13" baking dish with cooking spray. Set aside.

ABOUT CITRIC OILS

Both lemon and orange peel contain oils that protect the fruits from attack by fungi. These same oils—limonene and geraniol—have been found in one major study to inhibit tumor growth. (Because of their pleasant aroma, these oils are also commonly used to scent household cleaning agents, and they are useful as solvents.)

Research is under way to understand the tumor-fighting qualities of the oils and also to determine whether their benefits can be realized by drinking fruit juices that include ground rind.

Even the pulp may be beneficial. Orange and lemon pulp contains pectin, and one study found that modified citrus pectin inhibited the spread of prostate tumors in mice. The significance of this for humans is under study.

2. Place all ingredients except the vanilla bean in a large mixing bowl.

3. If using the vanilla bean, split it lengthwise and scrape the seeds into the mixing bowl, using the edge of a sharp knife. *Save the pod to flavor a sugar (add it to your sugar container) or wrap it well and freeze it to use in another recipe.*

4. Mix all the ingredients well. Pour mixture into prepared cups or pan and bake in preheated oven until just firm, about 1 hour.

YIELD: 8 TO 12 SERVINGS

Per serving: 214 Calories, 2.2g Fat, 0.2g Saturated Fat, 0g Cholesterol, 5.1g Protein, 45g Carbohydrate, 0.8g Fiber, 72mg Sodium

STRAWBERRY SHORTCAKE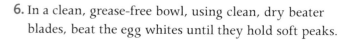

CAKE

2³/4 cups cake flour

1 cup natural cane sugar

2 teaspoons baking powder

1 teaspoon baking soda

1 cup 1% vanilla soy milk

1 cup unsweetened applesauce

¹/2 cup nonfat egg substitute

1 tablespoon vanilla extract

2 egg whites

2 pints fresh strawberries

canola oil cooking spray

CLOUD NINE FROSTING

1 cup natural cane sugar

¹/4 teaspoon cream of tartar

2 egg whites

¹/4 cup water

1 tablespoon vanilla extract

TO MAKE THE CAKE

1. Preheat oven to 350°.

2. Prepare two 9" cake pans: Cut a piece of wax paper or parchment to fit the bottom of each cake pan. Place the paper in the pans and spray the pans and the paper with cooking spray.

3. In a medium mixing bowl, sift together flour, sugar, baking powder and baking soda.

4. In a large bowl, mix together soy milk, applesauce, egg substitute, and vanilla.

5. Pour the dry ingredients into the wet ones and stir by hand or beat until no lumps remain.

6. In a clean, grease-free bowl, using clean, dry beater blades, beat the egg whites until they hold soft peaks.

7. Fold beaten egg whites into batter. Divide the batter evenly between the prepared cake pans.

8. Bake in preheated oven until a toothpick inserted into the center of each layer comes out clean and cake does not feel sticky when lightly touched, about 35 to 40 minutes.

9. Remove to racks and cool before removing from pans.

TO MAKE THE FROSTING

1. Place all the ingredients in a metal mixing bowl set over a saucepan of simmering water. (*The bottom of the bowl should not touch the water.*)

2. Beat on low speed with an electric mixer for 4 minutes. Increase to high speed and beat another 4 minutes.

3. Remove from heat. Beat 3 more minutes.

YIELD: 3¹/2 CUPS

TO ASSEMBLE CAKE

1. Rinse strawberries, cut off stems and slice half of them in quarters lengthwise. Reserve the whole strawberries.

2. Frost 1 layer of cake and cover with sliced strawberries, reserving about 20 pieces. Place the second layer on top.

3. Frost sides and top of cake Place whole strawberries on top with the cut-off ends nestled into the frosting.

4. Place remaining sliced strawberries in a border around the bottom of the cake.

YIELD: ONE 9" LAYER CAKE (10 SERVINGS)

Per serving: 318 Calories, 0.8g Fat, 0.1g Saturated Fat, 0g Cholesterol, 5.4g Protein, 72g Carbohydrate, 2.3g Fiber, 290mg Sodium

BROWNIES WITH COCOA GLAZE

These are so chewy and moist you will swear they are real fudge brownies. For Chocolate Orange Brownies, add 1 teaspoon grated orange zest and 2 teaspoons of orange extract to the batter. For Banana Chocolate Brownies, replace the applesauce with banana purée.

BROWNIES

2¼	cups natural cane sugar
1½	cups all-purpose flour
1½	cups low-fat cocoa powder
1½	teaspoons baking powder
1½	teaspoons baking soda
⅛	teaspoon sea salt
1⅓	cups unsweetened applesauce
1	cup low-fat silken tofu (8 ounces)
¾	cup 1% cocoa soy milk
2	egg whites or ¼ cup nonfat egg substitute
2	teaspoons vanilla extract
½	cup raisins (optional)
	canola oil cooking spray

GLAZE

1	cup low-fat cocoa powder
1½	cups rice syrup, liquid fruit sweetener or honey
2	teaspoons vanilla extract
1	vanilla bean, optional

TO MAKE BROWNIES

1. Preheat oven to 350°.

2. Sift sugar, flour, cocoa powder, baking powder, baking soda and salt into a large mixing bowl.

3. In a food processor, combine applesauce, tofu, soy milk, egg whites and vanilla and process until smooth.

4. Stir tofu mixture into dry ingredients until there are no lumps. Gently stir in optional raisins.

5. Lightly spray a 10" x 15" baking dish with cooking spray.

6. Pour mixture into prepared dish and spread evenly.

7. Bake in a preheated oven until a toothpick inserted in the center comes out clean, about 45 to 55 minutes.

8. Cool in pan before glazing.

TO MAKE GLAZE

1. Place all ingredients except vanilla bean in a food processor fitted with a metal blade and blend thoroughly.

2. If using vanilla bean, split it lengthwise and use a sharp knife to scrape seeds into mixture. Process again for 30 seconds. (*Reserve vanilla bean pod to flavor another recipe; wrap it airtight and freeze.*)

3. Pour glaze over brownies. Cut into 2" x 2" pieces. Serve.

YIELD: ABOUT 30 BROWNIES

Per brownie: 158 Calories, 0.9g Fat, 0g Saturated Fat, 0g Cholesterol, 2.7g Protein, 35g Carbohydrate, 1.7g Fiber, 114mg Sodium

CRISPY BROWN RICE COOKIES

You can use this recipe to make a Banana Split Log. Shape the prepared cookie dough into 2 logs about 3"x 8" each. Bake the logs at 350° about 25 minutes, until done. Prepare a recipe of Cocoa Glaze (page 102) and spread about $\frac{1}{4}$ of the glaze over one of the baked logs. Layer thinly sliced bananas on top of the glaze. Cover with the remaining log and pour the rest of the glaze over the top. Allow the glaze to run down the sides, as well. Decorate the top with thinly sliced strawberries and serve with a dab of Cloud Nine Frosting (page 96). To slice the log, use a large chef's knife or cleaver to make quick, heavy cuts.

> 2 **egg whites**
>
> ½ **cup maple or natural cane sugar**
>
> 3 **tablespoons maple syrup or honey**
>
> 2 **teaspoons vanilla extract**
>
> 3 **cups crispy brown rice cereal (preferably salt-free)**
>
> ⅓ **cup all-purpose flour**
>
> 1 **teaspoon cinnamon**

1. Preheat oven to 350°.

2. Place egg whites in the bowl of an electric mixer and beat on high speed until frothy. Turn down to low speed.

3. Slowly add sugar, while beating on low. Then increase to high speed for 2 more minutes. Stop beating.

4. Add maple syrup and beat on high speed for 6 more minutes. At this point, the mixture should be the consistency of meringue.

5. Add vanilla and beat 1 minute more.

6. In a medium mixing bowl, combine brown rice cereal, flour and cinnamon.

7. Gently fold dry ingredients into wet ingredients. Try not to deflate the egg whites.

8. Line a large baking sheet with parchment paper. Use a soup spoon to drop half-dollar-size mounds of batter onto sheet about 1" apart.

9. Bake in preheated oven until light brown and slightly firm to the touch, about 20 minutes.

10. Allow to cool 20 minutes before removing from baking sheet. Use the tip of a sharp paring knife to loosen cookies from the baking paper.

YIELD: **30 COOKIES**

Per cookie: 96 Calories, 0.1g Fat, 0g Saturated Fat, 0g Cholesterol, 0.6g Protein, 11g Carbohydrate, 0.1g Fiber, 20mg Sodium

DEVIL'S "FOOL" CAKE WITH COCOA FROSTING

This healthy chocolate cake will fool you. For variety, use Cloud Nine Frosting (page 96) instead of cocoa frosting. Or for a rich double chocolate cake sensation, make 1 recipe of Old-Fashioned Chocolate Pudding (page 109), but add a teaspoon of natural gelatin (agar) while cooking the pudding. Use this to fill and frost the cake. Or try baking the cake in a bundt pan; this version requires no frosting.

CAKE

- **3** cups natural cane sugar
- **2** cups all-purpose white flour
- **2** cups low-fat cocoa powder
- **2** teaspoons baking soda
- **2** teaspoons baking powder
- **4** egg whites
- **1¼** cups low-fat silken tofu (10 ounces)
- **1¾** cups unsweetened applesauce
- **1** teaspoon vanilla extract

FROSTING

- **2** tablespoons low-fat cocoa powder
- **¼** cup hot water
- **3** egg whites
- **1½** cups natural cane sugar
- **1** teaspoon cream of tartar
- **2** teaspoons vanilla extract

TO MAKE THE CAKE

1. Preheat oven to 350°.

2. Sift together sugar, flour, cocoa powder, baking soda and baking powder. Place egg whites, tofu, applesauce and vanilla in a food processor and purée.

3. In a large mixing bowl, combine tofu mixture with dry ingredients. Beat with an electric mixer until smooth.

4. Lightly spray sides and bottom of 2 round 10" layer cake pans. Divide batter between pans.

5. Bake in preheated oven until a toothpick inserted in center of cakes comes out clean, 50 to 60 minutes.

6. Cool on racks. Remove from pans.

TO MAKE THE FROSTING

1. In a large metal bowl, dissolve cocoa powder in hot water.

2. Add egg whites, sugar and cream of tartar. Set the bowl over a saucepan of simmering water. (*Water should not touch the bottom of the bowl.*)

3. Using a hand-held electric mixer, beat mixture on low speed for 4 minutes. Increase speed to high and beat an additional 4 minutes.

4. Remove from heat. Beat on high 3 minutes longer. Stir in vanilla and chill 20 minutes before using to frost cake.

YIELD: 4 CUPS OF FROSTING, ENOUGH TO FROST TWO 10" LAYERS.

TO ASSEMBLE THE CAKE

1. Place 1 layer on a serving plate. Frost top of layer.

2. Place second layer over first. Frost sides of cake. Frost top.

DECORATING NOTE: grind fat-free cocoa cookies in a food processor. Pat crumbs around the side of the frosted cake. Next, dip some beautiful summer fruits in egg whites and then in sugar; allow to air dry for 30 minutes. Arrange crystallized fruits atop the cake. (*The fruits are meant to be merely decorative; don't eat them, since they contain uncooked egg whites.*)

YIELD: ONE 10" LAYER CAKE (16 SERVINGS)

Per serving: 335 Calories, 1.4g Fat, 0.1g Saturated Fat, 0g Cholesterol, 6.2g Protein, 76g Carbohydrate, 3g Fiber, 270mg Sodium

TOFU CHEESECAKE WITH A FRESH BERRY TOPPING

This is as close as you can get to a real deli-style cheesecake without wandering into dangerous territory. For Chocolate Orange Cheesecake add $\frac{1}{2}$ cup low-fat cocoa powder to the mix and increase maple syrup to 5 tablespoons.

CRUST

- 20 individual fat-free graham crackers (about 1 cup)
- 1 egg white
- 2 teaspoons honey

FILLING

- 2 pounds or 2 blocks low-fat silken tofu (4 cups)
- 2 egg whites or $\frac{1}{4}$ cup nonfat egg substitute
- $\frac{1}{4}$ cup raisins
- $\frac{1}{4}$ cup orange juice
- 3 tablespoons maple syrup
- 1 teaspoon grated orange zest
- 1 teaspoon vanilla extract
- $\frac{1}{2}$ teaspoon orange extract
- $\frac{1}{2}$ teaspoon cinnamon
- 1 vanilla bean, optional
  canola oil cooking spray
- 1 recipe fruit topping (see below)
- $\frac{1}{4}$ cup fat-free graham crackers, for garnish

FRUIT TOPPING

- 2 teaspoons cornstarch
- 2 tablespoons apple juice
- 8 ounces frozen berries
- $\frac{1}{4}$ cup fruit sweetener
- 1 cup fresh berries (raspberries, blueberries or strawberries)

1. Preheat oven to 350°.

2. Spray a 9" round cake pan and line the bottom with a piece of parchment or wax paper cut to fit.

3. In a food processor fitted with a metal blade, process graham crackers to make fine crumbs.

4. Add egg white and honey and process until dough begins to come together to make a ball.

5. Press dough into bottom of prepared cake pan. Wipe out processor work bowl.

6. Place tofu, egg whites, raisins, orange juice, maple syrup, orange zest, vanilla and orange extracts and cinnamon into work bowl and process for about 2 minutes.

7. If using vanilla bean, split it lengthwise with a sharp knife and scrape the seeds into the tofu mixture. Process for 1 more minute. (*Reserve vanilla bean pod to flavor another recipe; wrap it airtight and freeze.*)

8. Pour batter over the crust and bake in preheated oven until cheesecake is slightly firm to the touch, about 1 hour. Cool and then chill.

9. Press graham cracker crumbs into the side of the cooled cake. Spoon fruit topping over the top. Chill until ready to serve.

TO MAKE TOPPING

1. Dissolve cornstarch in apple juice.

2. Place frozen berries in a saucepan with sweetener and bring to a boil.

3. Add dissolved cornstarch and boil until thick, about 2 minutes. Remove from heat.

4. Stir fresh berries into thickened mixture.

YIELD: ONE 9" CAKE (8 TO 10 SERVINGS)

Per serving: 163 Calories, 1g Fat, 0.2g Saturated Fat, 0g Cholesterol, 8.7g Protein, 56g Carbohydrate, 3.6g Fiber, 103mg Sodium

BANANA CREAM PIE

This is so delicious and authentic-tasting that I never hesitate to serve it in place of the traditional high-fat version. Instead of bananas, you might substitute strawberries, raspberries, mangos or whatever fruit you prefer. To make Crème Brûlée, reduce flour to ½ cup and divide finished pastry cream among 4 individual custard dishes. Coat the top of each custard with natural sugar and brown under the broiler until sugar bubbles— a very impressive fat-free dessert.

3	cups 1% vanilla soy milk
¾	cup sifted all-purpose flour
½	cup natural cane sugar
¼	teaspoon sea salt
1	vanilla bean, optional
¾	cup nonfat egg substitute
1	tablespoon vanilla extract
2-3	bananas (*to cover the bottom of the pie*)
1	recipe-baked Graham Cracker Crust (page 107) with the following change: when rolling the dough, roll into a 12" circle; fit dough into a 10" pie pan
1	recipe Cloud Nine Frosting (page 96)

1. Place soy milk, flour, sugar and salt in a saucepan.

2. If using vanilla bean, split it lengthwise and scrape out seeds into soy milk mixture. Add pod.

3. Place the pan over medium heat and bring to a boil, stirring constantly. Turn down to a simmer and cook until mixture begins to thicken, about 5 to 6 minutes.

4. Remove custard from heat. Stir a small amount of the hot mixture into the egg substitute, then return this tempered egg mixture to pan.

5. Place mixture back over heat. Continue to stir constantly and cook another 3 minutes or until custard thickens to a pudding consistency. Remove from heat.

6. Add vanilla extract and transfer mixture to a mixing bowl. Place a layer of plastic wrap directly on the surface of the pastry cream to prevent a skin from forming.

7. Refrigerate at least 1 hour.

8. Before assembling the pie, remove vanilla bean pod.

9. Slice bananas thinly on a diagonal. Place slices in a layer in the baked pie shell.

10. Spread cooled pastry cream evenly over bananas.

11. Spread frosting over pastry cream, drawing it up into little peaks. Serve.

YIELD: ONE 10" PIE (12 SERVINGS)

Per serving: 308 Calories, 0.6g Fat, 0.3g Saturated Fat, 0g Cholesterol, 6.2g Protein, 68g Carbohydrate, 1.6g Fiber, 197mg Sodium

OLD-FASHIONED CHOCOLATE PUDDING

Taste this chocolate pudding and you'll swear it's the real thing. Both my 74-year-old mother and my 4-year-old daughter love it. To make a Chocolate Cream Pie, use the Graham Cracker Crust (page 107), but prebake the crust. Fill it with this pudding mixture and use Cloud Nine Frosting (page 96) as a topping in place of whipped cream. Or top the pie with fresh raspberries or strawberries for a Chocolate Berry Pie.

- **2 cups 1% cocoa soy milk**
- **¼ cup natural cane sugar or fructose**
- **3 tablespoons cornstarch**
- **2 tablespoons low-fat cocoa powder**
- **1 teaspoon vanilla extract**
- **1 vanilla bean, optional**

1. Place soy milk, sugar, cornstarch, cocoa powder and vanilla extract in a saucepan.

2. If using vanilla bean, split it lengthwise with a sharp knife and scrape out the seeds.

3. Place seeds and pod in the pot with the soy milk. Cook the mixture over medium heat, stirring constantly until the begins to thicken to a pudding-like consistency, about 15 minutes.

4. Remove from heat and extract the vanilla bean pod.

5. Pour pudding into 6 individual cups or 1 large bowl and chill at least 30 minutes before serving.

YIELD: **6 SERVINGS**

Per serving: 105 Calories, 1g Fat, 0.2g Saturated Fat, 0g Cholesterol, 1.3g Protein, 22g Carbohydrate, 0.4g Fiber, 51mg Sodium

MAPLE FLAN

over 60 minutes

To make a Pumpkin,
Sweet Potato or Banana Flan, add 1/2 cup of strained vegetable or fruit purée to the custard mix. When corn on the cob is in season, I sometimes add 3/4 cup of fresh corn kernels to the custard and then garnish the flan with pomegranate seeds.

- 2 **cups maple sugar or natural cane sugar, divided**
- 6 **tablespoons water**
- 2 **cups 1% vanilla soy milk**
- 1½ **cups nonfat egg substitute**
- ¾ **cup low-fat silken tofu (6 ounces)**
- 2 **tablespoons tapioca flour or cornstarch**
- 1 **tablespoon vanilla extract**
- 1 **teaspoon maple syrup**
- 1 **vanilla bean, optional**

1. In a heavy saucepan over low heat, cook 1½ cups sugar and water, stirring occasionally, until sugar becomes a golden color, about 5 minutes.

2. Pour this caramelized sugar into 8 individual custard cups or 1 large soufflé dish. Turn the dish and tilt it so that the sides and bottom of the dish become coated with the caramelized sugar. Set aside.

3. Preheat oven to 350°. Fill a shallow baking pan ¼ full of water (*to make a* bain marie).

4. In a blender or food processor, combine soy milk, egg substitute, tofu, ½ cup sugar, tapioca flour, vanilla extract and maple syrup. Blend until smooth. If mixture has tiny lumps, pass it through a fine sieve to remove them.

5. If using the vanilla bean, split it lengthwise using a sharp knife and then scrape the seeds into the mixture. (*Save the bean pod to flavor another recipe; store it well-wrapped in the freezer; or put it in a sugar or maple syrup container to add flavor to those ingredients.*)

6. Pour mixture into prepared custard cups or soufflé dish and place them in the *bain marie*. Bake in preheated oven until custard is just firm, about 1 hour to 1 hour and 15 minutes.

7. Remove from oven and allow to cool before unmolding flans. Do not unmold until ready to use. If necessary, heat a sharp, pointed knife under hot water. Dry the knife and run it around the edges of the flan to loosen before unmolding.

YIELD: **8 SERVINGS**

Per serving: 241 Calories, 0.6g Fat, 0.1g Saturated Fat, 0g Cholesterol, 5.5g Protein, 54g Carbohydrate, 0.6g Fiber, 106mg Sodium

THE HEALTHY PANTRY

The first rule of stocking a healthy pantry is to buy organic ingredients whenever possible. That way you avoid preservatives, pesticides and other additives. To determine what is and isn't in a product, read the label carefully (page 59).

Many grocery stores now stock organic produce, but a natural-foods store may be a better source of condiments, canned goods, grains and juices. If you can't find ingredients locally, try contacting one of the national companies at the bottom of this page. Remember, this list is just a starting point for a well-stocked pantry.

CONDIMENTS

- balsamic vinegar
- barbecue sauce
- brown or white rice vinegar
- Dijon mustard
- fat-free soy mayonnaise
- ketchup
- low-sodium tamari
- mirin (*Japanese sweetened rice wine*)
- pickles
- raspberry vinegar
- sauerkraut
- umeboshi plum vinegar (*Japanese vinegar made with salted sour plums*)
- Worcestershire sauce
- yellow mustard

PRODUCTS IN CANS AND JARS

- applesauce
- crushed pineapple or pineapple chunks
- fat-free baked beans
- fat-free vegetable broth (*or fat-free vegetable broth powder or bouillon*)
- green chilies
- lemon juice
- low-sodium diced tomatoes
- organic corn kernels
- plum or prune purée
- tomato paste
- low-sodium tomato purée

BEANS AND GRAINS

- air-pop popcorn
- arborio rice
- barley
- black beans
- brown basmati rice
- brown rice (*short and long grain*)
- green lentils
- jasmine rice
- kidney beans
- navy beans
- pinto beans
- white rice

FLOURS, THICKENERS, POWDERS AND CEREALS

- arrowroot
- baking powder
- baking soda
- cake flour
- corn flour
- cornmeal
- cornstarch
- fat-free bread crumbs
- fat-free brown rice crispies
- low-fat cocoa powder
- oat bran
- oat flour
- oatmeal
- potato flakes
- potato starch
- rice flour
- soy protein isolate powder – plain, chocolate.
- tapioca flour
- unbleached flour
- whey powder
- whole-wheat pastry flour

SWEETENERS AND DRIED FRUITS (MANY OTHERS ARE AVAILABLE)

- apple juice concentrate
- brown rice syrup
- dried cherries
- fructose
- Fruitsource
- honey
- liquid fruit sweetener
- maple sugar
- maple syrup
- molasses
- natural cane sugar
- raisins

ESSENTIAL SPICES, SEASONINGS AND EXTRACTS

- canola oil cooking spray
- chili powder
- chives
- course black pepper
- cream of tartar
- dried basil
- dried oregano
- dried tarragon
- dried thyme
- granulated garlic or garlic powder
- granulated onion or onion power
- ground cinnamon
- ground cumin
- ground ginger
- ground nutmeg
- lemon extract
- medium-grind black pepper
- orange extract
- red chili flakes
- sea salt
- Spike seasoning
- turmeric
- vanilla beans
- vanilla extract

SOY PRODUCTS FOR THE REFRIGERATOR AND FREEZER

- 1 percent soy milk: plain, vanilla, cocoa
- Edamame (*frozen soybeans*)
- fat-free ground soymeat
- fat-free soy burgers
- fat-free soy cheese – mozzarella and Monterrey jack style
- fat-free soy deli slices
- fat-free soy sausage
- fat-free tofu hot dogs
- fat-free vegetarian Canadian bacon
- low-fat soy parmesan
- low-fat tempeh bacon
- low-fat tofu – firm, soft and silken
- white miso

MAIL OR PHONE ORDER

- **Natural Living Center**
  Offers vitamins, bulk foods (*including flours*) and foods for special diets. Catalogue available.
  Phone: 207 990-2626
  Web: www.acadia.net/natural/
  E-Mail: wgeiger@acadia.net

- **Asian Grocery**
  For spices, flours and chutneys from India and Pakistan. Web site includes recipes on how to use items like cumin seed, cardamom and turmeric.
  Phone: 312 453-0679
  Web: www.asiangrocery.com

- **East Earth Trade Winds**
  Chinese herbs for medicinal and cooking use. Catalogue available.
  Phone: 800 258-6878

- **Take Care**
  For soy protein isolate powder, flavored and unflavored.
  Phone: 800 445-3350

- **Harvest Time**.
  Specialized Japanese products, including miso, plum paste and soy milk.
  Phone: 800 628-8736

INDEX

AFTERWORD

Donald S. Coffey, Ph.D.
President, the American Association for Cancer Research
Professor of Urology, Oncology, Pharmacology and Molecular
Sciences, Johns Hopkins Hospital, Baltimore, Maryland

The old saying "we are what we eat" has proven true. And modern scientific insights now add, "What we eat may either cause or prevent cancer." It is clear that many people harm themselves with foods their bodies were not designed to handle.

HOW DOES FOOD CAUSE OR PROTECT US FROM CANCER?

Many chemicals formed within our bodies as we metabolize food can cause cancer. Many natural factors in food can neutralize these bad chemicals. What do we know about this battle of good and bad chemicals?

To metabolize food to form energy, we must use the oxygen we breathe. This essential oxygen combines with food to make energy, carbon dioxide and water. In this process, a small amount of oxygen is activated into a very hazardous form, known as reactive oxygen species, or ROS. The ROS forms of oxygen are free radicals that can damage the DNA. Damaged DNA is a central culprit in causing cancer.

Many foods contain natural antioxidants that can neutralize ROS. The body also has its own defense mechanism for knocking out both ROS and any carcinogens absorbed from our environment of air, water and food. The human body's defense system is made of enzymes that attack and destroy carcinogens and ROS. We know that in prostate cancer the defense system has been turned off, deactivated. Dietary factors can activate these defense enzymes.

HOW DID WE LOSE OUR WAY?

The first life forms on earth appeared more than three billion years ago. Two hundred million years ago, the first breast-feeding animals appeared, and at the same time males developed prostates. To this day, the breast and the prostate respond similarly in their variations in the incidence of cancer. If a country has a low rate of prostate cancer, like Japan, it also has a low rate of breast cancer; countries like the United States have high rates in both cancers.

About 70 million years ago, many species developed, including primates. More than three million years ago, the early relatives of humans appeared, walking upright and hunting and gathering. About 400,000 years ago, humans built the first fires. Modern humans appeared about 200,000 years ago, and their diet has evolved ever since. In the last few centuries the human diet has changed much faster than the human body—and our bodies are paying the price.

HOW DID OUR DIET CHANGE?

The great apes are primarily vegetarian, consuming great quantities of vegetables that are high in fiber. Later, some learned to eat raw red meat torn from the bones of other animals. This supplied a rich source of energy high in fat. Our ancestors developed weapons and learned to hunt, and much later they learned to cook meat over fires and to add concentrated fats and oils.

Eventually humanity wound up with five-star restaurants that saturated our foods with butter, along with fast-food restaurants and deep-fat frying. Collectively we now consume great quantities of meat soaked in fat, smoked and cooked or preserved with chemicals. This modern diet clogs our arteries and causes cancer. These fat molecules also get oxidized and interact with ROS and free radicals to form compounds dangerous to our health. Because modern food is often tasty and quick to prepare, it spreads throughout the world, and as it does we can track changes in cancer and circulatory problems.

WHAT SHOULD WE DO?

Like a fine car, the body needs to be maintained (no trade-ins are allowed). What is urgently needed are new eating and cooking habits. We should make use of diets that have evolved over the length of human experience, avoiding the fats of both fancy restaurants and fast-food chains. We must eat plenty of fresh fruits and vegetables and fewer overcooked fat-laden meats. We must have antioxidants in our diet, and we need to exercise and keep our spirits up. We may be tired of hearing these truths: it is your body and your choice.

Of course, in fighting disease, early detection is essential. People need to have check-ups. Just as a smoke detector provides early warning of a fire, a PSA test provides early warning of prostate problems.

Scientists around the world, many of them working with support from CaP CURE, are working to identify both the "culprits" and "heroes" within our foods and helping to define the body's natural defenses and how we can boost them. This research is essential to determine exactly what is best to eat, how it affects us and why. I wish for you the very best in your personal quest for good health and spirit. It is a noble challenge.

ABOUT CaP CURE

CaP CURE, the Association for the Cure of Cancer of the Prostate, is a non profit 501c(3) public charity dedicated to finding cures or controls for prostate cancer.

CaP CURE-supported scientists are discovering solutions to the problem of prostate cancer by investigating:
- Tumor molecular biology
- Chemotherapies that destroy cancer cells and halt metastasis
- Genetics that may help stop the disease at its earliest stages
- Apoptosis, or enhancing programmed cell death
- Vaccines and other stimulators of the immune system
- Gene therapies that are targeted to normalizing or eliminating cancer cells
- Anti-angiogenesis therapies that destroy a tumor's nutrient blood supply
- Treatments affecting the prostate cell's androgen receptor
- Radiobiology and radiology treatment
- Nutrition, vitamins and alternative therapies that may impede or reverse the progression of disease

CaP CURE also sponsors multi-center targeted research: a Gene and Family Studies Consortium that is unlocking the genetic mysteries of prostate cancer, a Therapy Consortium that is enhancing clinical trials for advanced disease around the country and a Nutrition Project that is studying the impact of diet on the disease's progression and recurrence.

With your help—and the help of others like you—CaP CURE will find a cure for the most frequently diagnosed cancer in America.

CaP CURE
1250 4th Street, Suite 360
Santa Monica, CA 90401
Phone: 310 458-2873 or 800 757-2873
Fax: 310 458-8074
E-mail: capcure@capcure.org
World Wide Web: www.capcure.org

CREDITS

We would especially like to thank the following
establishments for the use of their tableware and accessories;

Geary's
351 North Beverly Drive, Beverly Hills, CA 90210
310 273-4741

Tesoro
401 N. Canon Drive, Beverly Hills, CA
310 273-9890

Cottura
10250 Santa Monica Blvd, Los Angeles, CA
310 277-3828

Kirsten Zietz
Los Angeles, CA, 310 581-9023

Freehand
8413 W.3rd Stret, Los Angeles, CA
213 655-2607

Luna Garcia
201 San Juan Ave., Venice, CA
310 396-8026

ABOUT CaP CURE

CaP CURE, the Association for the Cure of Cancer of the Prostate, is a non profit 501c(3) public charity dedicated to finding cures or controls for prostate cancer. Prostate cancer is the most commonly occurring cancer in America, with a new case diagnosed every three minutes. To achieve its goal, CaP CURE has contributed more than $50 million in awards to more than 350 research projects in nine countries.

CaP CURE-supported scientists are discovering solutions to the problem of prostate cancer by investigating:
• Tumor molecular biology
• Chemotherapies that destroy cancer cells and halt metastasis
• Genetics that may help stop the disease at its earliest stages
• Apoptosis, or enhancing programmed cell death
• Vaccines and other stimulators of the immune system
• Gene therapies that are targeted to normalizing or eliminating cancer cells
• Anti-angiogenesis therapies that destroy a tumor's nutrient blood supply
• Treatments affecting the prostate cell's androgen receptor
• Radiobiology and radiology treatment
• Nutrition, vitamins and alternative therapies that may impede or reverse the progression of disease

CaP CURE also sponsors multi-center targeted research: a Gene and Family Studies Consortium that is unlocking the genetic mysteries of prostate cancer, a Therapy Consortium that is enhancing clinical trials for advanced disease around the country and a Nutrition Project that is studying the impact of diet on the disease's progression and recurrence.

In 1998, it is estimated that 184,500 American men will learn they have prostate cancer. The disease also affects countless wives, parents, children and friends. It costs the United States about $9.5 billion annually in medical care and productivity losses.

For Faster service:

Call toll free: 877-884-LIFE

Fax order to: 508-583-9904

E-mail order to: capcure@cfsmail.com

With your help—and the help of others like you—CaP CURE will find a cure for the most frequently diagnosed cancer in America. Here are some ways you can help:
• Purchase another *The Taste for Living Cookbook* for a friend, relative or colleague.
• Make a gift in honor or memory of someone special. Ask two friends to do the same.
• Encourage friends, family and business colleagues to contribute to CaP CURE instead of giving holiday, birthday or anniversary gifts.
• Participate in workplace giving that will match your contributions to CaP CURE.
• Designate a portion of your company's profits to CaP CURE.
• Provide in-kind goods or services.
• Volunteer your time and ideas.
• Host a fund-raising event for CaP CURE.
• Participate in CaP CURE's Home Run Challenge with Major League Baseball, the SENIOR PGA TOUR for the CURE or any of the many other CaP CURE fund-raising programs.

CaP CURE funds research to find cures or controls for prostate cancer. The organization does not offer medical consultations or advice. For information about the diagnosis or treatment of prostate cancer or other cancers, please call the National Cancer Advisory Service, sponsored by the National Cancer Institute: 800 4-CANCER.

YES! Please send me another copy of The Taste for Living Cookbook.
Price: $27.50 plus $4.00 handling charge. Total: $31.50
For six or more copies please deduct 20% from the cover price.
Add $4.00 handling charge for each book ordered.

Total Books ordered _____ x $27.50 _____

Less Discount − _____

Plus handling Charge ($4.00 per book) + _____

TOTAL _____

Name (*please print*) _____

Organization _____

Street _____ City _____

State _____ Zip/Postal Code _____ Country _____

❑ Check/Money Order enclosed, payable to CaP CURE (US funds drawn on a US bank)

❑ Mastercard   ❑ Visa

Card Number _____ Expiration Date _____

Signature _____

TTFL-01

NO POSTAGE
NECESSARY
IF MAILED
IN THE
UNITED STATES

BUSINESS REPLY MAIL

FIRST-CLASS MAIL PERMIT NO. 4 WEST BRIDGEWATER MA

POSTAGE WILL BE PAID BY ADDRESSEE

CaP CURE Books
PO Box 339
West Bridgewater, MA 02379-9970

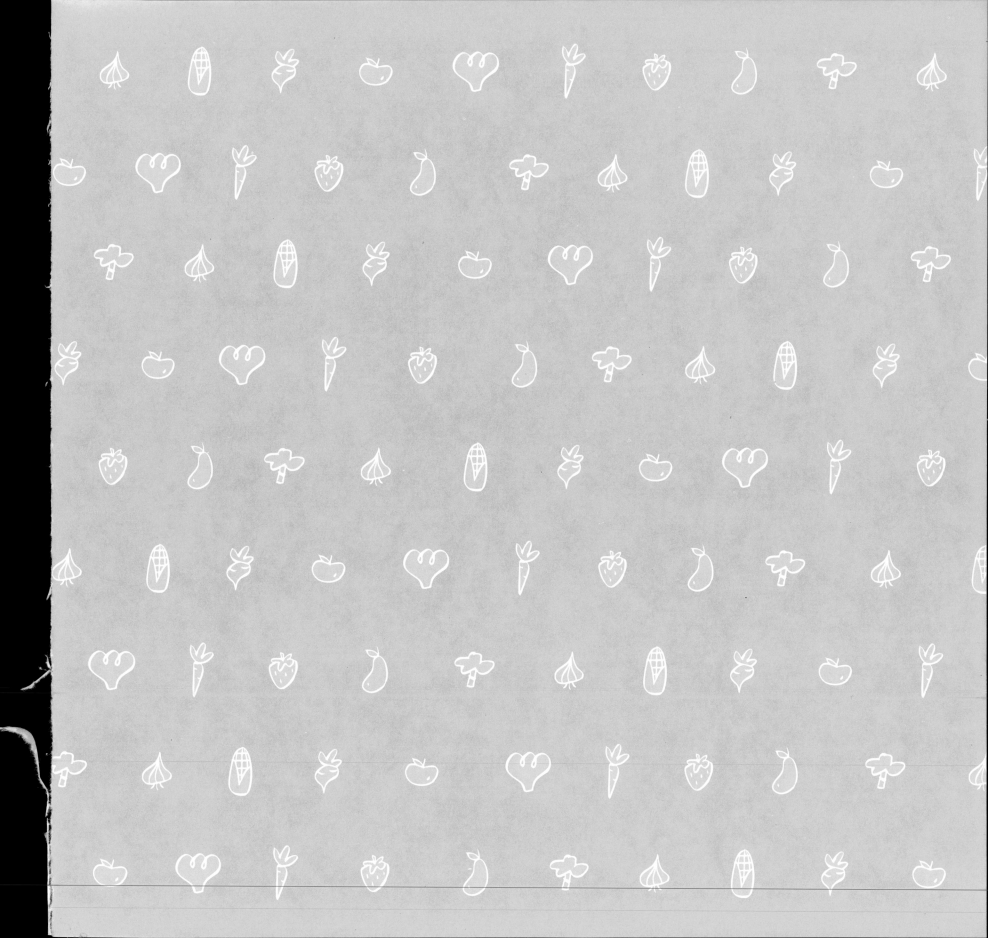

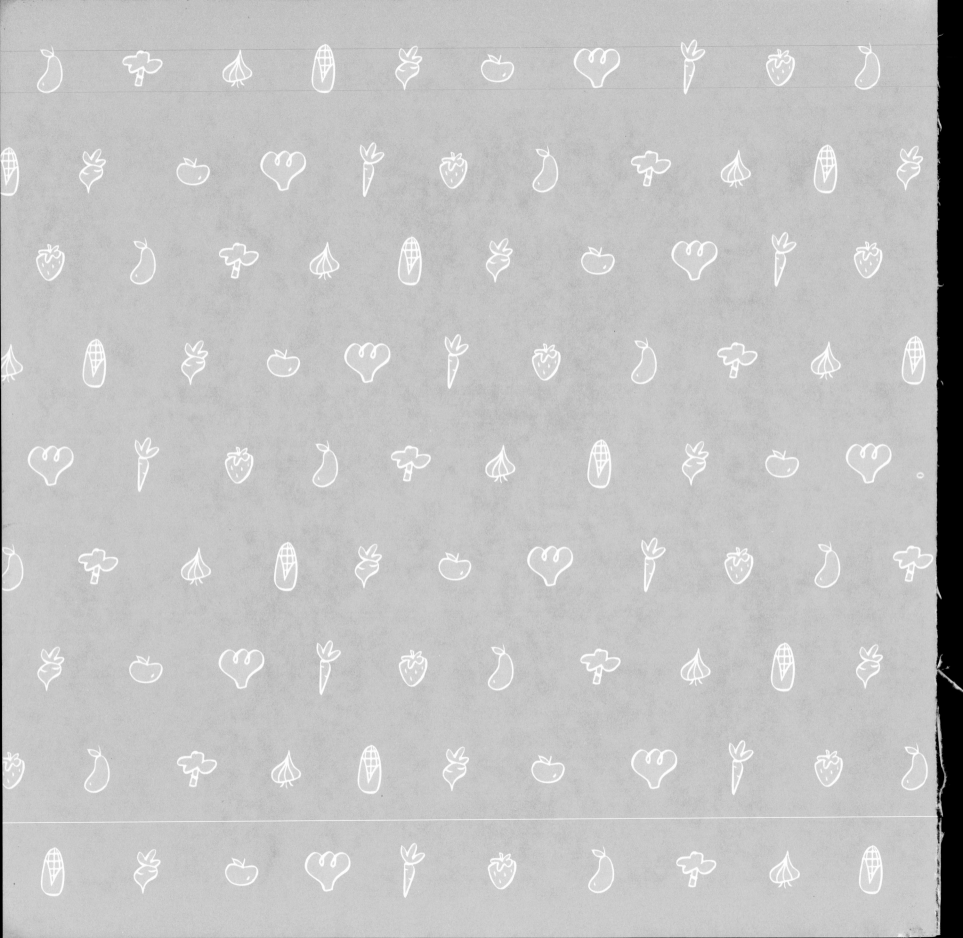